Free Mother to Good Home

A Handbook & Survival Guide
for Good Parents, Stepparents & Grandparents

who find themselves unappreciated, under–loved
& overwhelmed

by:

Kay Taylor

BALBOA.
PRESS
A DIVISION OF HAY HOUSE

Balboa Press books may be ordered through booksellers or by contacting:

Balboa Press
A Division of Hay House
1663 Liberty Drive
Bloomington, IN 47403
www.balboapress.com
1-(877) 407-4847

ISBN: 978-1-4525-4003-0 (sc)
ISBN: 978-1-4525-4004-7 (hc)
ISBN: 978-1-4525-4002-3 (e)

Library of Congress Control Number: 2011917814

Balboa Press rev. date: 12/13/2011

Inspiration

This book, in all its humanity and imperfection, is dedicated to my friend Jenny, a successful, intelligent, radiant, funny/fun-loving and caring woman, mother, and grandmother who, in the prime of life, on a beautiful spring day, having reached the end of her rope and after clinging to it as long as she could, ended her own life.

None of Jenny's friends or neighbors saw it coming; consequently, you could have knocked me over with a feather when I heard the news. I was in a state of utter shock and disbelief. As the reality set in, more painful and stunning facts came to light in the days following my friend's suicide. Jenny, I learned, had been estranged from her adult children for over a decade. And although she never spoke of it and came off as a strong and self-reliant woman who was completely in charge of her life, hidden away in a place where only Jenny could see and feel it, was the personal agony of a mother's broken heart. Her estrangement from her children was a painful and constant companion which reminded Jenny daily of all that she had lost and could no longer embrace and it tormented her.

The first time Jenny tried to kill herself it was more of a cry for help, for acknowledgment of her pain. Gerald, her husband of seven years, called Jenny's adult children with the news of their mother's attempted suicide. They were surprisingly indifferent and did not reach out to her. Her children's rejection was yet another crushing blow to a wounded heart already buried in pain. When Thanksgiving came along Jenny's suffering worsened, and again, my friend wanted to leave her pain. More determined this time, Jenny waited until her husband left for the day and then went to her bedroom and swallowed a bottle of pills. Gerald returned home to find his beloved wife near death. 911 was called and Jenny's life spared a second time. As he had done before, Gerald called and left numerous messages with Jenny's children, this time begging them to reach out to their mother. He pleaded with them to show mercy to her, explaining that what she needed more than anything was their love and support. For Jenny, it was literally a matter of life and death. Sadly and incredibly, they did not respond to any of Gerald's pleas for help. They did not return any of their stepfather's calls. Whatever the catalyst for and context of the family estrangement no one knew for sure, all that was certain was that it was powerful and impervious.

Winter had set in by the time Jenny returned home after her state-mandated hospital stay and follow-up therapy. My friend seemed to be her old self again and at peace with her life. No one, not even her husband Gerald would have a clue as to what was really happening in her heart and mind until spring of that year.

It was like any other morning—Jenny got up, poured her coffee and sat in her garden taking in the scents she loved so much. She cuddled her beloved poodle Archie; she even visited with neighbors. One neighbor recalled how tender and loving Jenny had been with her that morning and how she had made a point of embracing her before they parted. Gerald announced that he had to run a couple of errands and as he backed out of the driveway, he blew Jenny a kiss. She smiled and quietly went inside the house, climbed the three flights of stairs to her bedroom, took a gun and shot herself in the head. It was over—the estrangement and pain had finally come to an end.

Gerald suffered unspeakable trauma and pain as a result of Jenny's suicide, and again, he dutifully called his step-children, but this time, it was with the news that their mother was dead. This time, Jenny's children returned Gerald's calls, but tragically, it was too late for Jenny and too late for them.

As the story was related to me, I could not wrap my mind around how anyone could ignore a fellow human being's cry for help, especially ones own mother. An overwhelming sadness and grief filled my heart whenever I thought of Jenny. While attending Jenny's memorial service, I recall seeing her adult children there and wondering why they would come *now*. Hadn't they consistently ignored their mother's (and Gerald's) pleas for their love and support over the course of the last six months and perhaps for years? Other than Jenny's estate, there seemed to be no other plausible reason for them to fly to Florida and attend a service for a woman who they had repeatedly rejected over the past decade.

All the stories I heard about Jenny at the memorial described a loving, adventurous, and caring mother. Her children showed no outward signs of grief or distress but rather, seemed to carry themselves as if they were attending a mandatory business meeting. As the evening wore on, I found myself, along with other of her friends, judging Jenny's children and feeling both fiercely protective and indignant on Jenny's behalf. A combination of sadness and regret were my dominant emotions, and as I allowed myself to feel them fully, I had an epiphany. Perplexed by Jenny's ability to freely share with me the emotional wounds and scars she carried as a result of an overbearing and abusive mother, I was broken-hearted when I realized that she always put on a good front relative to her children. Perhaps it was because it was too painful to go to that place, or maybe it was pride, denial, or a combination of the two; I don't know. All I do know is that I was overwhelmed by Jenny's sudden and tragic death. My friend died too early in life and in my opinion, unnecessarily. Additionally and ironically, Jenny's death had occurred at the same time that I too, was immersed in my own drama, grief, and pain surrounding my relationship with my adult child. Like Jenny, I was experiencing tremendous heartache but dared not share my most vulnerable and personal wounds with others. It was while I struggled to absorb the shock and sadness of her suicide, as well as accept the reality of her loss that I began to see parallels in our lives and it scared me.

I decided two things then and there—First, that I would not end up like Jenny; that I would never allow my pain or the pain inflected on me by others to take over my life and destroy it. Second, I made a commitment that my friend Jennifer's life and especially her death would not be in vain, that she would not be forgotten. I did not want this extraordinary woman to be reduced to a regret or footnote in someone's personal history; nor was it enough that her life and story become a cautionary tale in the annuals of parenting. Jenny was so much more than that. I wanted something good, something hopeful and helpful to others to come from this tragedy. I knew then that I wanted, in fact, *needed* to do was reach out to all the wounded mothers out there who feel that perhaps their world has ended because they are currently estranged from their child or because they are entrenched in an unhealthy or even abusive relationship with their adult children. I want mothers to know they're not alone and that we can all honor Jennifer and mothers like her by finding our strength, re-creating, and empowering ourselves as strong, self-respecting woman, and by learning how to set proper boundaries and by then lovingly maintaining them. We are meant to live our life to the fullest, not endure it.

We can all learn how to get the love and respect we crave and deserve, even if it ultimately comes from a source other than our children.

Dedication

I dedicate this piece of my life and the lives of the parents who courageously shared their feelings and their stories to all the mothers, fathers, and grandparents who did the best job they knew how, and who, after giving it their all and raising their children (often alone) now find themselves alone, confused, and suffering. I also dedicate this book to our children—my children, Jenny's, and yours.

I dedicate this book to my children because, like you, although I don't understand them at times, and in spite of the fact that they can hurt like no other, I love them dearly and would give my life for them without a moment's hesitation. It is my prayer and hope that this book will provide a bridge across which both parents and children can one day pass or at least, meet in the middle; and with some luck, perhaps arrive at a healthy understanding, appreciation, respect, and acceptance of each other. I do not include *love* in that description because, although it may seem absent at times of pain or crisis, genuine-authentic love cannot be destroyed, only buried under layers of misunderstanding and pain.

Acknowledgments

I wish to acknowledge and thank my husband and best friend Neil for his support throughout the years and during this journey. Without his patience, love, encouragement, and support, this book would not be possible. I also want to thank and acknowledge my friend and the sister of my heart—Robin Pearce. Robin enthusiastically believed in me and in this book without reservation, and for that, I owe her a great debt of gratitude. To my friend and mentor Marianne Billington, my deepest love and gratitude. And finally, I acknowledge every mother, father or grandparent holding this book. We are all human beings first; all members of one family. And in the end, we are all here to learn, grow, connect, and contribute.

Contents

Introduction

I am not a doctor or a psychologist, nor do I have a PHD that follows my name; I have accomplished something that in my estimation and experience is far greater, more qualifying and much more enduring—I am a mother. As a mother, I share with you that although there are many-many things that I will never fully grasp or perhaps even have a clue about in this lifetime—

These things I know . . .
And I bet you do too

There has never been a moment when I did not love my children with all my heart. There was never an occasion when I chose another before my children, not myself or my health, not my husband, not my friends, neighbors, not hobbies, partying or other self interests, not even my job. My children were my entire life and identity.

Like you, as a mother—I gave selflessly and generously. I played heartily. I climbed trees with my children and read stories to them. I watched Disney movies, played ball, roller skated and skateboarded with them. Shed happy tears filled with bliss and pride at ballet recitals, and when no father stepped up to the plate, I learned the rules of baseball and became a t-ball coach and team mom all at the same time. I hosted countless parties, endured Chuck E. Cheese and happily cleaned up colossal messes. I celebrated with my children, prayed for them, and laughed with them. I tried to teach them right from wrong. I made mistakes with them, but never intentionally or maliciously. I grew up with them. I cried with them. I sheltered them. I held them close. I listened to them. I taught them all I knew about life. I encouraged them. I protected and defended them fiercely. I mended their wounds and was there for every doctor's visit, immunization, every stitch, every bruise and boo boo, and I caught every tear. I gave them money when I had it, rewarded good grades, and bought them the toy or shoes they just 'had to have'— even when I didn't have the money to spare. Like many parents, I raced to six different stores looking that specific gift they just had to have for their birthday or for Christmas because that's what they had asked Santa for; I happily endured the crowds and madness, and never complained. I was the *only mom* among dozens of dads at my son's Cub Scout meeting. I snuck away from work to my child's schools in order to catch a glimpse of them at school functions and performances. I worried myself sick on their behalf and waited up for them when they came home late. I tolerated and tried to be gracious during the challenging tweens and turbulent teens. I forgave them often and was quick to ask for their forgiveness when I had erred. I was always, and in all the ways I knew how, unconditionally there for them. I loved then and continue to love them fiercely and forever. I am a mother.

O

Their innocent, impressionable childhood years are now a thing of the past, and as I reflect back, I ponder the life I shared with my children and wonder why it is that more and more, I have come to see and believe that a large percentage of mothers end up on the short end of the stick at the end of the day. I have tried to wrap my mind around my own family's dysfunction and pain for years. I have also, over the course of time, blamed myself, beaten myself up, suffered immeasurable regret, pain and even depression because of the of the loss and estrangement I've experienced when my children have been disrespectful, unappreciative, or have taken their love or approval away. In retrospect, I am simply a mom who, perhaps like you, thought she had done everything right but who later blamed herself when life wasn't perfect for her child. I, like many mothers, felt guilty or responsible when my child acted-out or behaved badly, even when the bad behavior was aimed at me. I tried tirelessly to fix and please because, as I saw it, that was both my job and my pleasure. And when seasons arose in life when I was no longer needed, acknowledged, or appreciated as I had once been,

I felt profoundly wounded and lost—abandoned. My immediate response had always been to please, fix or rescue. Little did I know that I was in for a big surprise and awakening because this time, rather than my children, I discovered that it was *me* I needed to rescue and ultimately transform.

○

I have read and studied dozens of books on parenting, family, relationship dynamics, sociology and personal growth, and have attended women's groups and seminars, as well as other personal growth oriented training. I have sought insights through family counseling, and have committed myself to exploring the world of mothers by interviewing dozens of them in order to find out what we share in common, what we've done right, what we've done wrong, what drives us, as well as what wounds us most and how we can heal our wounds and our lives. One important reality for the parents of adult children to embrace is that their primary job of *parenting* is done. Good or bad—the cookie has crumbled and the chips have fallen where they may, and now it's time to examine where you're at, how you got there, and how to move on to a happier and healthier place both for you and for your child's sake. It is my hope that the anecdotes and insights shared in this book will resonate with you, inspire you, and lead you to a place of growth and healing.

A dear friend of mine who is a very wise woman and mother once shared some sage advice with me when she uttered a simple but profound truth. When being berated by her adult children for not living up to *their* expectations of her, she simply replied:

"This is my first lifetime too!"

Our children would do well to consider that from time to time.

CHAPTER 1

Know That You're NOT Alone

Advent of the E-Generation

"Making the decision to have a child is momentous.
It is to decide to forever have your heart go out walking outside your body."
—Elizabeth Stone

The very first thing you need to do is take a deep breath, pat yourself on the shoulder or give yourself a big hug and know that you're not alone—you are definitely not alone.

If you're reading this book that means you are a sister, an exclusive member of an ever expanding, very special group of women who are conscientious, caring mothers who did the very best job of child-rearing they knew how, and often did it alone, and yet, today are in pain. Perhaps you've been rejected altogether or (what is sometimes worse) you've become a subject in your child's kingdom, a mere pawn, or at least that's how it feels to you. If you've ever felt as if you've done it all, given your all, been everything for your child and still you sit waiting patiently, hoping and praying for their respect, reciprocation, or even a crumb of attention to fall your way, then this book was written for you.

The pain you're experiencing may have started as a spark which ignited an ember and burst into a flame that then grew into a three-alarm fire that can consume your heart and mind if you allow it to rage on. This emotional inferno has the potential to break your spirit and wound your soul if you let it. Although the source of ignition for this emotional wild fire varies, the pain remains the same for us all. Your teenager or adult child has perhaps moved away and is no longer in your life geographically or physically, maybe they have moved away from you socially or emotionally, or perhaps all of the above. They may be indifferent to you. They may be verbally or physically abusive or they may be neglectful. They may be emotionally ill and acting out; he or she may be narcissistic and totally self-absorbed to the point where you feel utterly insignificant. Your child may be involved in crime or drugs, be in jail or prison, or deceased. Absent death, the reasons for adult child/parent estrangement or abandonment are as varied and as deep as the levels of pain and dysfunction that create and often sustain the condition.

Whatever the reason for your pain, I can promise you one thing—the grief and suffering remains the same and can become crippling if allowed to grow like a cancer in your heart, mind, body, and soul. Our goal is to identify and hopefully stop the raging fire in its tracks, eradicate the pain, and once and for all, understand and end needless suffering. I hope you're in, but first let's see just how normal, or shall we say prevalent your situation and feelings are.

While writing this chapter, I took a break to watch the local evening news. The headline story was relevant, as well as captivating and disturbing. The story involved the daughter of an affluent couple in Naples, Florida. The young lady was a senior in high school; an honor roll student who had been accepted into several Ivy League colleges. As the story went on, I learned that this high school senior desperately wanted a sports car, and she wanted it *now!* The seventeen year old went to the car dealership to purchase the vehicle on her own and when she discovered that she did not qualify, she called her mother and demanded she come to dealership and purchase the car for her. Clearly, this young woman was feeling very entitled and empowered as she confidently embodied the role of authority figure in her relationship and communications with her mother.

When mom put her foot down and said *"No,"* the young honor roll student took matters into her own hands, literally. The seventeen year old who had never been in trouble either at school or with the law, now enraged by her mother's refusal to comply with her dictates, secured a 9mm gun, went home, tied her mother to a chair and held her at gun point demanding that she buy the car. She pistol-whipped her mother across the face, mercilessly beating her until, under threat of death, her mother agreed to buy the car. It was then that mom was taken at gun-point to the dealership where the transaction was completed.

The young woman's mother was so terrified of her daughter that she did not call the police that day, nor did she call that night. As a result of her overwhelming fear of her own daughter, and indeed fear for her very life, this mother waited until her teenage daughter went to school in her brand new sports car the following day before calling the police. After contacting law enforcement, this terrified and humiliated mother related how the child that she loved, bore, raised and nurtured had made demands of her and when they were not met, savagely beat her and threatened her life. The police immediately drove to the school and arrested the abusive teenager but this family's shocking and unhealthy behavior did not stop there.

Because this mom was hard-wired the same way all good mothers are—to love and protect our children unconditionally, she did not want to press charges. This mother loved her daughter and did not want to 'ruin her future.' Mom forgave her daughter and out of the absolute depths of her sorrow and brokenness, this mother *still loved* and *still* wanted what she thought was best for her daughter. That is an incredible love. Or is it? While we can all recognize and identify with the concept of unconditional love and sacrifice, we must also acknowledge that at times, it expresses itself at a tremendous cost. I'm sure this mother is haunted not just by the memory of the hellacious beating she suffered at the hands of her own daughter but also by the equally haunting reality of a broken heart and broken dreams— the shattered illusion of the *perfect family* and total destruction of the inherent assumption of reciprocal love, respect, trust, and safety within a family. Mixed in with it all, comes the perplexing and painful questions—*What did I do wrong? Did I help create this monster?*

Ironically or perhaps prophetically, after hearing this disturbing local news story, I randomly flipped channels and landed on a national cable news station where the story being broadcast was that of yet another young adult-daughter who had verbally abused, assaulted, and then threatened the life of her mother. The young woman in this story was in the midst of a heated and very contentious custody battle with her mother, who the courts had awarded temporary custody of the young woman's baby to. What the videographers captured on film was a daughter physically assaulting her mother and using the most deplorable and frankly unimaginable language during the course of the verbal assaults on her mother. The grandchild, an innocent toddler, had become a pawn in this young woman's vendetta against her mother. It was gut-wrenching to watch the exchange. As a mother, it was mind-numbing and heart-breaking to watch these two stories back to back and try to make sense of them as I labored to digest the images, words, and sounds I had just been witness to. I could not for the life of me wrap my mind around the social dynamics that define many parent/adult child relations today.

All this begs the question—Why? Why is there an epidemic of disrespect, reckless verbal abuse, and entitlement among this nation's adolescents and young adult population? Why has this aberrant behavior escalated to its current levels and beyond, to levels of physical abuse and sadly, at times, culminating in death or murder within what was once a loving family—Why?

How did it get to be this way?

The extreme stories above are a statistical drop in the bucket to the realities of parental neglect, disrespect, and abuse now occurring at epidemic levels in this country. Research and multiple interviews with parents have uncovered a possible answer—an intersection in our culture where a collision of ideas, beliefs and values resulted in a major shift in our national identity, and more profoundly, forever changed what kind of children we raised. From the 80s onward, many children grew up either alone or unsupervised in a social atmosphere of dramatically increased exposure to the adult world, adult concepts and privileges, and entitlement, all of which heralded a generation of young people who possessed a sense of personal enlightenment, entitlement, power, privilege, and expectation of immediate gratification. At its worst, this shift resulted in children and young adults who now felt *equal to*, and often times, *superior* to their parents. I refer to this culture of children, teens, and adult children as the **E-generation.**

Parent after parent has described scenarios wherein their elementary school-age child came home and boldly proclaimed that they (the parents) no longer possessed the right to discipline them. I certainly recall the first time my child came home and laid down the new law of the land. I was made indelibly aware of the new rules of the house when my child was in the first grade. And while my child rarely if ever received a parental swat from me, I had been officially put on notice by a six year old. That day, there was a paradigm shift in our home and in our relationship that resulted in an imbalance in the authority structure in our home, and not only because my child had fully embraced their new role as power broker in their life but because I had surrendered it. Children were now empowered and encouraged to let their parents know *the way it was going to be*, and that, in my opinion, was one of the first evolutionary nudges that sent the dominos falling.

The subject of corporal punishment/spankings is hotly debated and is now considered abuse at all levels, and while I do not endorse spanking, the historical fact remains that nearly all baby boomers were raised with a completely different standard. In fact, up until the 1980s, not only was spanking a common practice, it was expected if a child misbehaved. There were very few *enlightened* parents who did not swat a hand or spank their children in those days. Despite what some liberal talk show hosts claim, *spankings* were not only considered normal, they were an accepted part of a national standard under which most children were raised. The fact was: spanking or putting a bar of soap in the mouth of sassy child was just part of the average American kid's life. Who will ever forget the movie A CHRISTMAS STORY or Ralph suffering *"soap poisoning?"* Not one person in the theater walked out in disgust or screamed—*"Abuse!"* In fact, they did the opposite—they laughed out loud because they identified with poor Ralphie. Today, audiences would probably be appalled, in fact, today, such a scene would more than likely end up on the editing room floor or never conceived of or shot in the first place.

One of the nation's most beloved and well-respected father figures is the legendary Bill Cosby. Bill Cosby is an incredibly gifted and bright man who not only has a doctorate degree in education but is also a successful actor, comedian, educator, author, and philosopher/commentator on American family life. After achieving success as a comedian, Cosby went on to become the quintessential father to an entire generation of Americans on the iconic television show—'The Cosby Show.' Cosby spoke and joked openly about life in America as he knew and remembered it as a child. We all remember his *Fat Albert* albums, as well as the famous phrase he repeated often when describing both being a child and being a parent—*"I brought you into this world and I'll take you out!"* How many of us joking (or not) heard that one as a youth?

Most shockingly, at least for anyone who isn't a baby-boomer and remembers those days (either fondly or with fear and anxiety), let me dare to reveal that there was actually a time, not only in private schools but in public schools as well, when corporal punishment (*i.e., spankings*) were regularly administered to disrespectful or unruly students. I know this because on one rarified occasion, I was one of those unruly students. It was the very last day of elementary school, and after being publically scolded and humiliated by my sixth grade teacher (wrongly, I might add) I was both angry and indignant, two emotions kids were just never permitted to feel, let alone express back in the dark ages. Throwing all traditional adult/child protocol out the window, I summoned every ounce of courage I had, and in one excited utterance, I told our teacher what every single sixth grader in the whole class secretly thought of her, including me . . . and I didn't do it under my breath (the accepted practice); I actually said it *out loud!* This was 1970, a time when children were not self-expressed, let alone outspoken, especially to their parents, elders, or authority figures of any kind. In fact, it was the polar opposite of times; it was a time when *children were to be seen and not heard.*

After my brave declaration, a deafening silence fell over the room as my disgruntled and flabbergasted teacher reached for a large phone mounted on the wall (part of a thing we used to call an intercom system). Hushed words were exchanged and when she got off the phone she barked the five words every kid dreaded the most—"*Go to the Principal's office!*"

Now for those of you who don't know what that meant back in 1970 and the years that preceded it, let me share. It meant that the principal (who always seemed to be a man back in those days) was going to verbally thrash you and then make you bend over and give you the spanking you had earned, deserved, and were now most certainly going to get. Not only was spanking an accepted practice, parents were usually pleased by the notion of an authority figure lending a helping hand in reprimanding their disrespectful or disobedient child. Many children from the 70s and earlier grew up hearing one of two things, or both if you came from a religious family—

1) *"spare the rod and spoil the child"* (a bible verse, no less).
2) *"This is going to hurt me a lot more than it is you."* (Remember that one?)

Whenever I heard those pearls of parental rationalization, I always begged to differ, not that it ever helped. And yes, it's okay to smile or to laugh if you're old enough to remember that time and those values in America. As Mr. Cosby himself is quoted as saying: *"Through humor, you can soften some of the worst blows that life delivers. And once you find laughter, no matter how painful your situation might be, you can survive it."* Bill Cosby also humorously noted that—*In spite of the seven thousand books of expert advice, the right way to discipline a child is still a mystery to most fathers and mothers. Only your grandmother and Genghis Khan know how to do it."*

The point is—back then, parents and their children were not peers and parents most certainly were not *friends* or *buddies* with their child. There was a personal, familial, and social structure and hierarchy in place along with an absolute expectation of respect and submission from children, period. Many parents, private school administrators, and even some public school teachers and principals hung the Ten Commandants on their walls and were quick to remind children that it was not just *their rule*, it was *God Almighty's commandment* that they honor their mothers and fathers. That was the established social standard and norm for baby boomers. The hippie generation challenged and forever changed that old paradigm. I wonder sometimes if any of those social/political rebel rousers of the late 60s and 70s who shook up and forever changed the landscape of America and traditional family values, ever look back at that time (perhaps as a result of becoming parents themselves) and question whether all that rebellion, freedom and re-definition and distribution of personal expression and power was such a smart idea to instill in our nation's youth. One thing is for sure, a few years later, when children became the authority figures in their own lives and homes when stay-at-home moms nearly became extinct because women either wanted to, or *had to* work, an entire generation of latch-key kids raised themselves.

Envision kids with no authority figures in their lives, no role models, no one at home, and then stack onto that the influence of cable television, MTV, the advent of computers, video games, a phone of their own in the house, or pagers (remember those?). On top of that, these same kids were being told that there were areas of their young lives where they could actually advise, supervise, and even dictate or demand certain behaviors from their parents. Ironically, they were taught this in the same public schools who used to spank them when they misbehaved; quite a paradigm shift. Again, I cannot emphasize enough that eliminating spanking in schools and teaching children to 'tell someone' when there is abuse at home via making it reportable was absolutely necessary and should be applauded. But, for those mothers and fathers who were loving, responsible, conscientious parents (and I believe that's the majority of parents) the way the program was sometimes introduced to our children, implemented and executed often had bad results for good parents.

For those of you whose blood pressure has flown through the roof and are already crying foul, let me assure you, I do not espouse corporal punishment/spankings that are tantamount to abuse, nor did I abuse my children; additionally, the parents interviewed for this book did not abuse or inappropriately discipline their children; that was not the demographic I was interested in. This book was *not* written for parents who abused their children either physically or emotionally. If you are such a parent, you need not read further because you need an entirely different kind of intervention and assistance that is not available to you in this particular book. ***Free Mother to Good Home*** was expressly written for the thoughtful, loving, nurturing parent who is now pained and bewildered by the end-relationship they are now experiencing with their teen or adult-child and wonders to themselves *'What in the world did I do wrong? What can I do now?*

Children brought up in this new era and atmosphere of social awareness, privilege, and expectation share similar beliefs and behaviors; they are best defined as the E-generation.

Enlightenment

Overexposure to adult concepts, images, privileges, etc.

Entitlement

Being taught and strongly feeling that they deserve the same rights and privileges as their parents and other adults or authority figures.

Empowerment/Emboldened

Not only do I deserve this, you owe it to me; it is my inherent right and I will, if necessary, demand and insist upon it.

Excess

Too much of everything, and getting it instantly creates a very hungry beast that can never be satisfied.

Expectation & Immediate Gratification

No longer experiencing and learning the art of patience, temperance, or *earning something over time* and/or via the application of goal setting, diligence and hard work.

Equality

When a child's psyche and lifestyle embody enlightenment, entitlement, excess, empowerment, and being emboldened, accentuated by a high degree of expectation and immediate gratification, they cannot help but feel equal to, and often superior to their parents and other adult authority figures.

As the father of modern psychology put it—*"Children are completely egotistic; they feel their needs intensely and strive ruthlessly to satisfy them."*—Sigmund Freud. If that was true when Dr. Freud first made the observation decades ago, it most certainly is true of E-generation children. Freud went on to say—*"All children lack the insight and maturity to consider anyone other than themselves."* I, along with a lot of other parents, not only agree with this statement but believe that E-generation children in particular are destined to experience major power struggles with their parents and other authority figures in their lives as a result of their strong sense of entitlement.

Hereafter, I will refer to children raised within this kind of environment and with these types of exposure as the E-generation; and trust me, there are some teens and adult children out there who really know how to put the *"E"* in—*M**E**-generation.* These children were not born within specified dates but rather, they are children born within a specified type of environment and with a tremendous amount of *"E"* exposure (as defined in the list referenced earlier). I end this chapter with an anonymous letter that has been published in many newspapers and online forums across the country and is a monument both to the past and to a way of parenting long since discarded, and in most cases, for good cause. And yet, ironically, many of the recipients of this brand of parenting are thankful for having received it. The old days and old ways verses the E-generation represent two extreme ends of a social/cultural/familial teeter totter where strict/consistent discipline sits at one end and the six "E"s at the other. In my opinion, both are unhealthy extremes, the middle ground is the healthiest place to be. Sadly, as a result of the dramatic shift that has taken place in the minds and lives of children and their parents, many adult-children, teens, and even younger children have assumed the role of authority figure in the family. And what have many confused and bewildered parents done in response? They have given up their role as parent and caved-in under the influence and pressure.

My Drug Habit

The other day, someone at a store in our town read that a methamphetamine lab had been found in an old farmhouse in the adjoining county and asked *"Why didn't we have a drug problem when you and I were growing up?"* I replied *"I don't know about you but I had a drug problem when I was young."*

I was drug to church on Sunday morning. I was drug to church for weddings and funerals. I was drug to family reunions and community socials and gatherings no matter the weather. I was drug to the park to pick up litter, so I'd learn to be environmentally conscious. I was drug by my ears when I was disrespectful to adults. I was drug back to the five and dime store to apologize if I ever dared to steal a candy bar. I was drug into a corner for a time-out if I disobeyed my parents, told a lie or did not speak with respect to my elders and authority figures. I was drug to the kitchen sink to have my mouth washed out with soap if I uttered a profanity. I was drug out to the yard to mow and pull weeds. I was drug to the homes of family, friends and neighbors to help out some poor soul who had no one to mow the yard, repair the clothesline, or chop some firewood. I was drug to old folk's homes to visit the elderly and be reminded of their importance and the respect I should show them. And for all the kindnesses and considerations I was instructed to exercise, if my mother or father suspected that I asked for a single dime as a tip for those kindnesses, I would have been drug back to return the money.

Those drugs are still in my veins and they affect my behavior in everything I do, say or think. They are stronger than cocaine, crake, or heroin; and, if today's children had this kind of drug problem, I believe America would be a better place.

God bless the parents who drugged us.
—an anonymous but thankful baby boomer

CHAPTER 2

When Adult Children Abandon, Abuse or Neglect Their Parents

Name Calling, Demanding/Demeaning & Other Unacceptable Behaviors

In so many cultures, the elderly are not only deeply respected but are deemed to be the culture's elite and valued for their years of experience, wisdom, and contribution, a far cry from the way many of our elderly are treated in America. Granted, there are exceptions; however, more than ever before in our nation's history, a disappointingly large percentage of the elderly are living alone in assisted living facilities, separated from their family with little or no contact from their children or grandchildren. Many of our elderly live out their last days in nursing homes, assisted living facilities, with friends or, in worst case scenarios, destitute and alone.

A hundred years ago, such neglect would be a social stain on a family's name and reputation, in fact, it was not uncommon for generations of a family to live together under the same roof, and not solely because they *had to* economically but more often than not because it was inherent in the family's culture and tradition, and intrinsic to its core values to do so. The practice is still common in many cultures around the world and in some subcultures in America but is seen least often in Anglo-American families. Compartmentalizing or discarding of our elderly is just another of our country's social/familial follies, a sort of culmination of the escalating and ever-changing shifts in our core values surrounding family. Aside from our elderly and their changing role in the family and in society in general, the role of adult children and grandchildren has changed radically too.

The problem with kids today

How many times have you heard a person over 40 years old say— *"When I was a kid, I would never dream of speaking to my parents the way kids do today"?*

I recall waiting in line at the local drug store with an older woman who appeared to be in her mid to late seventies. We engaged in friendly chit-chat as we waited. After witnessing a tween verbally scold her mother for refusing to buy makeup for her, and the mother relenting, our conversation turned to children and the staggering level of *'it's all about me-ism,'* as well as, what we older people identify as rampant disregard and disrespect among today's youth. Along with the indifference and down-right disrespect that is so prevalent among kids today, there appears to also be an absolute reckless abandon with which young people speak their mind and declare their opinions, and do so without censoring either their thoughts or their words. Some of today's E-generation youth will happily put you in your place and enthusiastically tell you just how *ill-informed, wrong*, or *inept* you are, and they'll do it while making spectacular demands of you at the same time. And if you are among the most unfortunate of parents, your E-generation child will top it off with an expletive or some other from over verbal abuse or threat. Ever been there and experienced that? If so, you're not alone. This type of behavior appears to be rampant among many of today's teens and young adults.

As the silver-haired woman and I continued our chat, I made a comment about just how much the times have changed and before I could finish my sentence, she perked up and snapped *"You aren't kiddin!—Why, if I spoke to my parents the way kids do today, I would have been wearing dentures before I got to high school!"* Although her remarks may startle or offend you, the raw honesty of her words echo the truth of many generations of Americans that came before this current age of enlightenment and entitlement. The E-phenomena also speaks to the major power shift in the mindset of teenagers and young adults in our culture.

Many of you may argue that episodes of parental disrespect have occurred throughout the ages. True, but here's one big difference that immediately comes to mind—it's called RESTRAINT. While getting reamed out or put in our place (rightfully or wrongly) most kids of my generation did one of two things—we either berated our parents safely within the confines of our own mind (silently but satisfyingly) or, if we were feeling particularly brazen, we calculated the risk, waited, and then, when the offending parent turned their back to walk away, we made our move. We indignantly mumbled our protests under our breath as our parent walked away, usually behind their back. Sticking out tongue out or making ugly faces with contemptuous expressions that were never actually seen by our parents was an alternative for the more creative, but never-never did we openly *talk back*, let alone offer a retort or instruction to our parents. In fact, the mere fantasy of doing so brought with it visions of the multiple and painful ways in which we would be punished if we ever dared such a suicidal feat.

Name calling, demanding/demeaning and other unacceptable behaviors

If you have never known the pain of having your child yell or scream a foul name at you, then count yourself blessed. Where before, it was simply not done, it appears to be in vogue today. Hell, many E-generation kids feel it's their *right* to freely express themselves, no matter how abusive or hurtful their words are. Some very aggressive and/or troubled children, many teenagers, and adult children berate, condescend, and speak harshly and disrespectfully to their parents on a regular basis.

Boundaries and parental lines drawn in the sand can vary. One mother may allow her adult child to lie to her, another adult child uses drugs and regularly steals from his mother and she puts her head in the sand as long as her child offers the pretense of formal respect when addressing her face to face; sadly they live in a world of lies and pretense. There are still other parents for whom the line represents verbal abuse; those are the parents for whom being called a name or hearing their child curse in their presence is absolutely forbidden. Although the trigger points vary, the problem is the same—the disrespectful/disparaging behavior of one's teen or adult children.

I remember thinking that what I was experiencing was perfectly normal and that all teenagers go through a rebellious stage that included hostility, arguing, challenging authority, and calling one's mother *"Bitch"* or saying *"F&@% you!"* in hateful tones. No wonder actor, author, and satirist Ed Asner once said *"Raising a kid is part joy and part guerilla warfare."* In my experience, I eventually became somewhat desensitized to the verbal assaults because at the time, stories were just beginning to emerge about teenagers cutting themselves and doing other harmful things to their bodies as a way of acting-out, so I recall being relieved that I was only being condescended to and cursed at. Little did I know—I was laying a very unhealthy foundation for my future relationship with my teenagers by being so passive about unacceptable behavior.

In addition to verbal attacks, some teenagers and adult children actually get physical with their parents or threaten to. When it comes to your safety, even the potential or threat of physical abuse must *never be tolerated*. Remember the mother from Chapter one whose daughter pistol-whipped her and then threatened to kill her, and yet, the mother in that story did not want to press charges against her 17 year old daughter. What message is that mother sending to her teenage child? What behaviors are going unchecked, or worse yet, are being rewarded or reinforced? How safe will that mother feel going into the future? How will that young woman manage her life and relationships in the future? Let's be clear—you are not loving yourself, your child, or protecting other innocent people in your community when you allow your child to act out violently. You must draw an absolute and immoveable line in the sand when it comes to physical violence. There simply are no exceptions to this rule, period! As life coach and media icon

Oprah Winfrey famously responded after hearing the news that a famous singer had *(allegedly)* viciously beaten his equally famous girlfriend—*"if they hit you once, they'll hit you again."* Incidentally, the young singing starlet didn't want to press charges either. Whether it's a boyfriend, husband, wife, or your own child, does not matter, what is at play in abuse situations like this is a heightened level of emotional imbalance and aggression that fuels a propensity for violence that must not be ignored or tolerated. You are not loving or protecting either yourself or your child by refusing to hold them responsible for their behavior. Remember, it was a lack of accountability and consequences that caused the problem in the first place and must now stop immediately.

It is imperative to remember that this book is for those parents who consciously did the absolute best job they could and did not abuse their children either verbally or physically. Furthermore, it is implied by your participation in reading this book that you did not willfully or maliciously berate your child, call them hurtful names, emotionally or physically abuse, neglect or abandon them. If a parent sets up the relationship to be abusive by their example, then it is very likely that the child will grow into the role modeled for them by their parent. The emotional/social math and evolutionary process is just that simple. But, what if you were/are a thoughtful and committed parent who generously gave love and support, and got something entirely different in return? What then?

When we set up the rules or lack thereof and it results in a major power shift with the child having free reign and control, then take control, they will. And like anyone suddenly placed in a position of absolute power and influence, the child will become either a loving and considerate governor of the estate or a selfish dictator and tyrant. Recalling Freud's thoughtful insights and observations about youth, what's your guess? Here's a hint—because it violates the natural order and because children lack the emotional maturity to govern themselves properly (let alone their parents) they often become the dictator of the house regarding all affairs relative to them. Once that domino falls, it's hard to recover because like all dominos, its collapse sets off a chain reaction within the family dynamic that can be socially, emotionally, financially and physically staggering in its magnitude.

It is never too late

It is never too late to draw a line in the sand, even if the misled/ abusive child in your life is now an adult. Exhibiting a lack of respect for yourself is like painting a big target on your back, or in the case of mothers, on your heart. The first healthy sign that you are establishing a sense of *'self'* rather than *utterly self-less mother* is that you will establish boundaries and lovingly maintain them. If you have younger children, set the rules in place early on, establish boundaries and consequences, and most importantly, you must be consistent, lead by your example, and when the rules are violated, there must be a consequence. My bet is, if you are suffering the slings and arrows of adult child abandonment, abuse, or neglect, you did not set boundaries early on, and if you did, you did not maintain them or establish and enforce effective consequences consistently when they were violated. You may have also brought your own emotional baggage into the mix. We'll address that aggravating factor as we move on.

You are not your child's *FRIEND*—You are their *PARENT!*

From my experience and research—one of the biggest mistakes I've observed parents make is to try to be their child's **friend** rather than their parent. When you decide to strive for friendship, you instantly surrender you role as parent. Your child's friends are their peers, their equals—*not you*—that's not your job! But, if you've unwisely chosen to be a peer, all parental boundaries, as well as the structure your child desperately needs have been traded off for an atmosphere of confusion and a potential for disaster, and why? Because you abdicated the parental throne and all its responsibilities and privileges; and now, now you are not just a wanna-be *friend,* you are a *peer.* And still it gets worse for you because along with ridding the child of a much-needed parent and role model via your volunteering to vie for the position of friend and peer, you've also now demonstrated to your child that you are no longer in control. In fact, the opposite has become true; by virtue of your need to please and your need to be accepted as a friend, accompanied by your neediness in general, you have now officially become *'less than'* in the eyes of your child. You are now not just a peer, you are a *needy* peer-someone who is desperately seeking their acceptance, love, and approval. And don't think that your child doesn't sense that *need* in you or doubt for a second that they will play on your need for attention, acceptance, love, and approval from them. Parental authority and respect are often the first dominos to fall, setting off a sequence of collapse that eventually escalates to a virtual avalanche of troubling behaviors which at best, conclude in heartache and isolation, and at its worst, ends in loss or tragedy for so many well-intentioned parents.

CHAPTER 3

When it's Not All Sunshine & Roses

How Some Disappointed E-Generation Moms & Dads Feel About Their Parenting Experience

This chapter comes with a warning and request:

READER BEWARE—I'M QUOTING
&
DON'T SHOOT THE MESSENGER!

I shared with you earlier just how strongly some of our older generation feel about the sense of self-empowerment and the freedom of self expression with which today's youth/young adults express feelings and thoughts that are often better kept to themselves. We also revisited the days of our youth, when children were to be seen and not heard and when mumbling under one's breath was the accepted standard for rebellion. Clearly, both being a kid and being a parent have changed dramatically since then. In my opinion, those roles have changed both for the better and in some cases, for the worse. When parents were asked about the status of their relationships with their adult children and if they'd do it all over again, the following unedited responses were given.

Gerald, a successful businessman in his early sixties:

"Yeah, I have two daughters. One is forty-one years old and the other forty-five. The younger one is a demanding bitch on wheels and the older one,

well, I guess she's an okay person; I don't really know because she just started talking to me last year."

Ronald, a fifty-six year old attorney:

"I have two children and I love them dearly, but, if I knew then what I know now, I would have raised dogs instead. They don't lie to you; they're loyal, and you don't have to listen to a litany of complaints, send them to college, or pay for a fairytale wedding, twice! I am an attorney and here's some free advice—get dogs!"

Xavier, a musician and father of four:

"I'm sure I wasn't a perfect dad but I loved my kids and I did my best. I just never imagined that I'd be fifty-eight years old, barely surviving on disability and all alone or that none of my children would have time for me. I suppose I have to develop a thicker skin and get used to the idea of being alone for the rest of my life. I just thought it'd be a lot different, that's all."

James, a retired Chief of Operations of a large international company:

"I have no children, in fact, in my early thirties, I ended an otherwise happy and healthy marriage with a beautiful woman because my wife decided she wanted children and I did not. I am sixty now and do not regret it for a minute, especially when I see the hell my friends and colleagues are going through with their kids. To be completely honest, I feel like I dodged a bullet."

Anne, a retired political lobbyist, writer, and mother of three:

"Yes, I believe I'd have children again. I'd just do everything differently because the thing I've learned over the years is this-you can do 999 things right, and I mean, to absolute perfection, but your child will seldom if ever recall those times or events. Oh no, it's that one time out of a thousand when you didn't perform perfectly or as they thought you should; it's 'that time' when you let them down—that's the time or act they remember; it's

also the one that defines you and marks you for life. *Trust me, I'm in my 70s now and can assure you that kids 'never' forget the times you failed them but seem to develop amnesia when it comes to the 999 other things you did right."*

Lauren, a fifty-five year old homemaker and grandmother:

"I know everyone says that if they knew then what they know now, they would never have had children. Well, I got that one beat. I wanta know where I go to give them back!"

Robert, a compassionate community leader and father of two:
"I hate to say it but I absolutely would not have children if I had to do it all over again. I love them with all my heart, but they also have broken my heart. I always seem to be sad, irritated, and worried or bailing them out of one kind of trouble or another, and they never seem to appreciate it. If I could do it all over again, for my 13th birthday, instead of asking for my first shaving kit, I would have asked for a vasectomy!"

Pauline, a Grandmother from Vermont that I met at Disney World while sitting beside her as she waited for her grandsons to exit a roller coaster ride

"I honestly don't know. I guess I say that because I don't know why, but my daughter became very hostile towards me in her teens. No matter how hard I tried, I could never do anything right. She's thirty-two, has two children of her own now, and it still hasn't changed a bit between she and I. I am almost always in a state of worry, afraid of setting her off and having her yell at me or ignore me."

★ Pauline leapt to her feet and quickly moved away from me the minute she saw her grandsons walking toward her after exiting the roller coaster ride. That was when she added:

"If she knew that I was talking to someone about her or about our relationship she would be furious with me. Honestly, I am intimidated by her and afraid of her getting angry at me so I can't talk anymore. Please be sure to change my name in your story."

Tom, an RN at a community hospital:

". . . My adult kids? I'll tell ya how serious I am—If I knew then what I know now, I would have intentionally exposed myself to radiation when I was an x-ray tech to ensure sterility. Hell, I would have stayed in the room with every single patient without wearing a lead-lined apron! Does that give you an idea?"

Ernest, an eighty-five year old retiree:

"Of course, I'd have kids again, they're wonderful but I'd warn people . . . my son is in his sixties and I'm still comin' to his rescue all the time. Lord knows what he will do when I pass on."

Antonia, a seventy year old mother of six, grandmother, and great grandmother visiting Florida from Puerto Rico

"Oh my, yes I would have all my children again. They call me every day and ask me to come to visit them all the time, and my daughter, my oldest, she has a room at her house especially for me. They are my blessings and bring me great happiness. But let me tell you my secret—you must bring them up right from the time they are very-very little or else you will be very unhappy."

Jacob, a very successful financial adviser and single parent

"I honestly cannot answer that question. I love my son but my life has become a living hell. There is always a battle being waged by his mother (my ex) about everything imaginable and unimaginable. She's constantly saying the most horrible things about me in an effort to make my son (eleven years old) hate me. I battle just to maintain his love and trust. And now, I'm reduced to being a 'Disneyland Dad'—unless I am entertaining my son or buying him extravagant gifts, he's bored with me and doesn't seem to have much use for me in his life. I just don't know what to do anymore. I feel lost!"

Jesse, a disabled, sixty-eight year old father of two adult daughters

"I love my girls to death but I do have to confess that they hurt my feelings all the time with their thoughtlessness. I don't think it's intentional on their

part, they just never seem to have time for me and don't include me in their lives unless it's convenient for them or unless they need me or my money for something. I know that they love me but I just wish I felt more respected and valued by them."

Kathryn, an accomplished professional & conscientious mother of two:

"I have to say, if I knew how it would all turn out, I don't believe I would have had children, at least, I'd think hard about all the responsibilities and consequences beforehand. I love my children very much, perhaps too much. But it's not just the pain a parent is likely to experience if their child is unappreciative or disrespectful, it's also the worry you suffer, wondering if they're okay, as well as the financial expense and the guilt you feel if you can't afford to give them the good life you'd like to or the things they want. In today's stressed-filled world, with school shootings, pedophiles, and disaster always looming in the air, I honestly do not believe I could do it again knowing what I know now. My love and worry for my children has become an emotional prison for me and I don't know how to get out."

David Finkelstein

"The mother of three notoriously unruly youngsters was asked whether or not she'd have children if she had it to do all over again; she replied "Yes, but not the same ones!""

Bill Cosby

"I guess the real reason that my wife and I had children is the same reason that Napoleon had for invading Russia: it seemed like a good idea at the time."

So why do I share these comments? One reason—if you have ever uttered the words *"I wish I never had children!"* or *"This is not what I expected!"* Or, if you have cursed your children for the pain they have caused you, even under your breath or in the privacy of your own mind, you now know you're not a horrible person and that you're also not alone. The people who shared their hearts above are all nice people, good citizens, and conscientious parents who gave it their all and did their absolute best. They were also brave enough to share that in spite of their best efforts, they often felt emotionally and financially drained and even a little jipped by their experience of parenting at times; it's okay to admit it, and it's okay to express your disappointed or hurt feelings. It's okay to be human.

All the parents interviewed above, with the exception of the single gentleman, expressed that they love their children and would do anything for them. These are all *good parents* who love their children but find that the conditions and outside influences under which many E-generation children grow up today can often make the likelihood of successful/rewarding parenting feel like a roll of the dice in Vegas, especially when one considers the level of social sophistication, entitlement issues, and lack of old-school manners that seems to permeates our youth.

Why is it we have children in the first place?

It would be historically inaccurate to say that it was easier to have children in the past; however, it is true that until the twentieth century, children were a necessity for most families in our country. They helped on the family farm or they worked in family businesses; they were always at the ready for their parents. Most families had rock solid values that were tried and true. And their kids? Well, their children behaved themselves and did as their parents instructed them to, even into adulthood.

Parents of generations past wanted their children to do better, excel further and accomplish more than they had. My own husband will readily admit that he had no interest in going to college and getting a degree in accounting, but that is what his very practical immigrant father thought was best for him. He never questioned his father's authority or the choices he made for his only son's life. I might also add that luckily my husband loves what he does and is very happy that at a time when others were *'doing their own thing'* and expanding their minds with drugs, he, out of respect and a sense of honoring his father, kept his nose to the grind stone, went to college and majored in a field his father knew would provide a good living for him, thereby insuring a better, more secure future. Accomplishing 'a better life' for one's child was the primary goal of most immigrant parents; it is also the dream for most home-grown parents of baby boomers as well.

Today we have children for a variety of reasons and sometimes they come as a complete surprise. I believe most people have children as a means of creating the love and emotional security they crave in their lives. Others have children as an extension of their ego, a sort of cure for mortality or they have them entirely by accident. Other children are brought into this world under the false belief that they will make a partner stay in a relationship or make a bad relationship better—seldom does that happen. Strange that you have to take a semester long course, pass a written test and then perform sufficiently to pass an actual driving exam before you are issued a driver's license in most states, but when it comes to producing and raising a human being, and knowing how to do it in a responsible and nurturing way, no such classes or qualifications are offered or required. When it's all said and done, and regardless of how babies were conceived and brought into this world, most parents love their children deeply and do the best job they can with the education, tools, and resources available to them. It is my hope and prayer that children will one day realize this simple truth and cut their parents a well-deserved break.

CHAPTER 4

All in the Family—Part I

Sons—Daughters—Adopted/Stepchildren-In-laws & Other Dysfunctional Family Relationships

Today, certain family dynamics have become a predictable cultural norm in our society; for example, it is common for fathers and daughters to get along better than mothers and daughters. Likewise, sons and their fathers are often at odds with each other while the son enjoys a relatively relaxed and supportive relationship with his mother, and not just during his youth, but well into his adult years. As an example, how many of you have witnessed an interview with a sports figure who has just accomplished an amazing athletic feat, set a record, won the Super Bowl, or an NBA championship? Most of the time, who do these macho men/ athletic heroes and icons of our culture invariably thank? *Their Mommas*—That's who! Why is that?

❖ Why are mother/son relations usually better than mother/ daughter relations?

❖ Why are fathers often hard on their sons while paradoxically they are powerless wimps and pushovers when it comes to their daughters?

❖ And most perplexing of all—Why are mother/daughter relations often the worst of the bunch?

Kay Taylor

Mother/Daughter—Father/Daughter Relations

Why are mother/daughter relationships sometimes strained during the teen years and sadly are often severely damaged, if not irreparably broken by the time the daughter reaches adulthood? What social/emotional dynamic is at play here? I believe it has a lot to do with mothers being the primary caregivers in our society and in our homes. Mothers are usually the one to establish and enforce the rules, and this, mind you, is a highly unpopular position to hold within a family. Additionally, often times, women, regardless of their age can be catty and competitive, even inside sibling-on-sibling or mother/daughter relationships.

Like it or not, when examined more closely and with a commitment to objective honesty, it's becomes clear that in our social/cultural history we have taught and reinforced some very undesirable skill sets in our daughters. Many fathers will readily admit that their little princess has them wrapped around their pinky. Little girls are taught at a very young age how to use the power of sweetness, accompanied by their cuteness, charm, and a smile to manipulate the world around them. And if that doesn't work, what other affect is then employed? It is the highly refined art of *'pouting'* or playing the part of the destroyed young maiden. The world has come to an end because she didn't get what she wants. What usually happens next? The parent involved in this particular production (usually dad) does what? They concede; they 'give in'; they fold like a deck chair; and what does this teach the child? It teaches them the single most important lesson they'll learn in their young female lives, and it's an unfortunate one—that pretending (whether it's to be sweet and charming, weak and helpless, or pouting and destroyed) will more often than not get them what they want. Any woman who is honest with herself knows this is true. Girls are taught early on to use their charm to get what they want. This talent is usually taught to them by another female, sometimes an older sister, aunt, or grandmother, but most often by their own mothers, who incidentally, are usually master craftswomen themselves.

The years fly by, and oddly enough, the very same behavior that was so beguiling and rewarding as a toddler and young girl, is now suddenly frowned upon, and by who? Usually it's the very same person who taught the behavior to them in the first place—mom. This creates quite the quandary doesn't it? Can you see a tad of conflict and confusion arising out of that predicament? And we wonder why daughters have such complex love/hate relationships with their mothers. And why shouldn't our young apprentices be peeved? After all, we not only know the manipulative/ helpless maiden game, we taught it to our daughters when they were adorable little toddlers. Most of the mothers interviewed admitted to possessing this skill set as well as to having employed it at one time or another in their life. We inherently know that this kind of manipulative behavior is wrong, and when our daughters get to an age when we no longer encourage or tolerate dramatic, manipulative, contrived or controlling behavior, we then become our daughter's rival, competitor or nemeses. Once that happens, at best, we are viewed as competitors for attention and power, and at its worst, we are perceived as our daughter's enemy. This is usually the time when there is a major shift or breakdown in mother/daughter relations.

Now this is not to say that ALL mothers teach their daughters to be artificial and manipulative. But in all honestly, how many of us mothers, at one time or another, encouraged our little girls to *"Go give daddy a kiss and tell him you love him, then ask for _____"* or maybe our daughters saw us model that behavior firsthand and then later rebelled when we set boundaries around the very behavior(s) they learned from us—behaviors they may still see mom engage in. I believe that nearly all women have employed this mechanism of control or manipulation at one point or another in their lives, even if only when they were young. For many of us, it was hardwired into our DNA when we were very young either by our mothers or some other female role model.

How some E-generation girls manipulate—a breakdown of their playbook

I am unapologetic for what (via numerous interviews and observation) in my opinion, is an overt style of behavior on the part of many young girls, tweens, teens, and young women, as well as adult women, all the way up to older women who should know better by their age. A great many females of nearly all ages (notice I didn't say *all* but a great many) in our cultures have learned/adopted a strategy when it comes to protesting and/or getting their way with others, particularly with their parents and members of the opposite sex. It is a predictable methodology that is artfully employed via implementation of the followings tactics—

1. **Sweetness, charm, hinting and/or manipulation**—*if you love me, you will . . .*
   Which, if not successful, is followed by:
2. **Pouting to outright sobbing and helplessness**—*I am so hurt, wounded or helpless—please rescue me.*
   Which, if not successful, is then followed by:
3. **Ultimatums, threats and tantrums**—*these are often unrelenting and amazing in how fast they manifest. A real artist can go from helpless tears into a full-blown tantrum complete with malevolent threats within seconds once they see plan 2 isn't working.*
   And . . . if that doesn't work—
4. **There is a withdrawal of attention or love, or a return to step one where the cycle starts all over again**.

If you doubt it, begin observing the behavior of young girls who desperately want something or are determined to have things *their way*, particularly teens. When this behavior/pattern isn't identified and corrected early on, it is then carried into adulthood where it is routinely employed—just ask any man.

Do boys behave this way too?

Although there are exceptions to everything, boys are not taught or encouraged to behave this way with adults, nor are their brains capable of it. They're just not wired the way we women are. I believe that is why they are much more forward and abrupt in their communications whereas girls/women are like onions; you have to peel through layers and layers of God only knows what before you get to the core of an issue, problem, communication, meaning, context, their feelings or their needs.

What about dad?

As for dads, truthfully, they are fairly simple emotional beings, and are generally known to be innocently clueless and easily manipulated by both the woman in their life and their children, particularly their daughters. The reasons are both clear and basic. Daughters generally bring all the pluses of female energy, love, validation, and adoration to a father without all the drama and conflict that a female contemporary or intimate relationship carries with it. In other words, they don't come with the baggage we grown women do, or so fathers innocently assume early on. Daddies simply adore their little girls and are beguiled by their sweetness and charm. This can last a lifetime and be experienced as either loving and rewarding or manipulative and destructive for one or all parties involved.

I share all this to offer a context around which we may begin to see some elements of similarities in our experiences with our children, and with our daughters in particular. I also share this knowing full well that there are mothers out there who, from start to finish, did their job of parenting ethically and selflessly, and with a tremendous level of integrity and good intentions. Mothers who sought to really teach their son or daughter what it means to be a caring, empathic, responsible member of the human race. And despite their efforts or perhaps because of them, their child or children rebelled and acted out in negative ways.

If you're identifying with some of the dynamics described here, take heart and remember—we're all in this together. This book is written by a member of the club, a mom who had high highs as a parent and experienced the lowest of lows too, who wondered why and asked the same painful questions, sought answers, did research, went for counseling, attended groups and seminars, and interviewed dozens and dozens of other mothers just like you, so let's forge on.

Father/Son—Mother/Son Relations

Father son relationships in America have become so stereotyped that they are fairly predictable, at least, they were for baby boomers. In the case of most boys born before the 1970s and certainly before the 60s, their fathers did not share tender emotions verbally, and they especially did not demonstrate them physically. For generations, American boys were taught that it was a grievous sign of weakness to cry. Furthermore, these young boys almost never heard the words *'I love you'* and they were seldom, if ever hugged or cuddled by their fathers. A hardy handshake was the order of the day; it didn't matter if it was a wedding or a funeral or your graduation, a son could expect a firm handshake from his father.

In the homophobic world in which baby boomers grew up, to be emotionally or physically demonstrative with one's son meant that a man was weak or gay (queer was the derogatory term used back then). The credo was—*'do not show tender emotions and do not touch another man affectionately, not even your son'*—it was a kind of silent code among homophobic men. Sadly, before the current age of enlightenment and acceptance, physical contact between males, even father and son was deemed inappropriate and therefore became a strictly enforced taboo. I am sure there were exceptions to the standard of conduct that existed for fathers and sons, but ask any man over the age of forty-five what they experienced with their fathers and most of them will confirm that the no emotion/ no touch Rule *of Conduct* was firmly in place throughout their childhood. Growing up and even into their adulthood, boys were almost never told they were loved or shown physically affection by their fathers and this went on for generations. Perhaps that is part of the reasons girls have always been able to manipulate their fathers, because fathers of that generation would allow themselves to feel and express love to their daughters. Just a thought . . .

In addition to the mores of the day, sons were often entrenched in an intense competition with the standards and goals their fathers had established as monuments to manhood and acceptance early on. This dynamic often resulted in sons being pitted against their fathers in a race to see who was the most masculine. How often do we still see scenes depicted in films where the father, aged and tired, must keep up with, or better yet, out-perform his young son, *show him up* and vice versa. Sons became doctors or lawyers because their fathers were doctors or lawyers, and it was expected of them. In the old days, sons many times didn't have much of a choice about their future profession or vocation; they simply were expected to follow in their father's footsteps. Although in my husband's case it worked out for him and he loves what he does, on the all in all, fathers dictating their son's future or sons feeling like they MUST follow in their father's footsteps is not positive, healthy parenting, nor is it healthy for a son to feel that he *must* attain a particular status or level of material success in order to win his father's love or approval.

The good news is, there has been a huge paradigm shift in father/son relations over the last two or three decades, with most fathers being emotionally secure and making it okay to touch and caress, cuddle and nurture their sons, while at the same time readily telling them how much they love and value them. Healthy love, touch, and positive reinforcement is something both sons and daughters need. By the way, it's a *human need* that doesn't stop at age eighteen, or twenty-one. The need for connection, significance, and love never ends, not for any of us.

Oedipus Smedipus & other relationship theories

We've all heard of the Oedipus complex. Admittedly, I'm just a mother of reasonable social, emotional, intellectual, and academic intelligence and do not hold a degree in Greek philosophy or history. That being said, we are not going to delve deeply into an ancient and twisted belief that states that on some level, sons want to sexually possess their mothers and kill their fathers. You may ask—who am I to question an ancient Greek philosophy that has survived centuries and has been reinforced by icons in psychology? Answer: I just a mother who raised a son and believes the mother/son connection is a lot less complex and polluted than that. After all, during our history, we humans used to think the world was flat and that it was okay to own other human beings—so much for the ancients.

Kay Taylor

One Mother's theory

Because, in the past, fathers have historically distanced themselves from their sons emotionally and physically, and with babies being babies, and children being children (i.e., needing and desiring connection and affection) the child (a son in this scenario) simply gravitates to the parent who exhibits the most readily available love and support; this person is almost always *mom*. Boom! Mystery solved.

Add to that the fact that, in the past, fathers were often more emotionally available to their daughters than to their sons and you have all the ingredients for an intra-family dynamic where the mother feels a need to compensate for dad's emotional unavailability, and therefore appears closer to the son. I say *'appears'* because, as any mother will tell you—mothers love their children completely and equally, and most mothers would die for their children in a heartbeat. Mothers who have both a son and a daughter do not love their sons more, in many instances, they are simply compensating for dad's lack of hands-on interaction with his son or his inability to be demonstrative toward his son while pampering and being available to the emotionally more accessible/safer child, his daughter. On top of that, there usually comes a time when that aforementioned mother/daughter dynamic (i.e., the alpha female competition) sets in, and with that, the typical American family portrait takes shape; and it looks something like this: the mother *appears* to favor the son and is critical of her hyper sensitive daughter, who may have dad in her corner and be at odds with mom and/or other siblings.

Because males are, or appear to be (in my experience) less complicated and a bit more easy-going, the male/son will get along with the unconditionally loving/supportive parent (mom), whereas the female (daughter) is often caught in the drama of female competition and conflicting values (i.e., what was taught, encouraged and rewarded as a child verses what exists now between she and her mother). End result—your typical American family, complete with sibling rivalry, mother/daughter drama, and dad on the outside looking in.

How all this plays out for mothers and their daughters

As a result of these dynamics, daughters, more often than sons, tend to feel unloved and unaccepted by their mothers. Where daughters surveyed reported that they feel criticized and even disliked by their mothers, sons generally reported the opposite feelings or opinions. It has been the experience of countless mothers, and is my opinion that—daughters who feel this way, do so, in part because they have allowed too many toxic emotions and/or conscious or sub-conscious female competition to clutter their view, inadvertently creating filters that do not allow them to recognize or feel their mother's love.

Ironically, after speaking to multiple parents, both fathers and mothers, it is clear that what daughters often imagine, feel, and embrace as their reality will ultimately becomes a self-fulfilling prophesy as more and more conflict is generated between mother and daughter, with the sad result being emotional safe-guarding and estrangement. Sons, on the other hand, have traditionally leaned on their mothers for support when their dads were breathing down their necks with the result being that they enjoyed a relatively relaxed and supportive relationship with mom. I believe, and it's been my experience that it is within these relationship dynamics that sibling rivalry sometimes emerges. It's all about feeling significant, loved, and cared about, and all too often, it turns into a competition between siblings.

Adopted children

Family therapists will tell you that most adopted children, regardless of their up-bringing or how 'balanced' their life and family, no matter how well they were loved, will experience what is called 'Original abandonment' to one degree or another. Whether or not this is true in all cases, I don't know, I can only speak to my own experiences as an adopted child, as well as my husband's experiences, as he too, was adopted.

For both my husband and I, issues of worthiness, trust, and subconscious fears of abandonment did show up in our respective lives in various ways. We each became *Super Pleasers* who were also overly generous to everyone around us. We wanted to make all the people within our reach happy and did so to a fault, at least on a superficial level. We sought to earn their approval and acceptance which often resulted in people taking advantage of our generosity. This character trait also made us incredibly tolerant of what most people would consider unacceptable behavior. That was how our particular abandonment issues played themselves out in our lives. Thankfully, we attended seminars, read veraciously, attended family and personal counseling, and gained tremendous insight into these areas and were subsequently able to establish healthy, satisfying boundaries and release abusive relationships.

By the way, when speaking about abandonment issues and how they anecdotally act-out in parent/child relationships, we will take a broad road. When referring to the 'abandoned child' or 'original abandonment,' that includes children who were abandoned by one parent and raised alone, the illegitimate child who grew up knowing they were unwanted or were the result of an accident, rape, or some other *less-than-optimal* circumstance, as well as the utterly forgotten in our society—foster children. All children rising from one or more of these origins of birth will inevitably carry with them certain kinds of emotional baggage (some small and insignificant, some large and imposing). As we explore these feelings and relationships, it's important to remember that carrying the baggage or scars of our past does not make us wrong, bad or inferior; it simply makes us human.

For such a thing as ORIGINAL ABANDONMENT and all its affects to exist, that must mean that its polar opposite must also exist—ORIGINAL LOVE—CONNECTION—SECURITY—NURTURING, and a sense of ABSOLUTE BELONGING. What a wonderful safety net to shield vulnerable young children from the emotional slings and arrows of life. For those that endure and survive childhood without that safety net beneath them, they know what it's like to face the world with the deck stacked against them emotionally and socially. It takes an extraordinary individual to overcome a pronounced case of original abandonment. I share that from both personal experience and from having grown up witnessing the effects of abandonment on the dozens and dozens of children that passed through our foster home without the benefit of having that safety net to embrace them when they were frightened or catch them when they fell.

My Adoption Story and Original Abandonment Issues

The news that I was not my parent's biological child came at an awkward age; it also came as a complete surprise to me. I was twelve years old and very secure in who I was and in the knowledge that I belonged right where I was; then it came—the utter destruction of my sense of safety and self identity. It happened on a cool summer evening in 1970 when my parents called me out of the water for a pool-side chat. Wrapped in a towel and shivering as we sat at the picnic table beside the pool, I was matter-of-factly told that I was not my parent's biological child. I recall going into an altered/dream-like state. They went on to say that the only reason they were telling me was because they worried that someone else in the family might inadvertently reveal the truth to me one day.

As soon as they finished, my parents said I was free to resume swimming. They casually announced they were going to the store, and with that, got up, turned their backs and walked away as I sat stunned, trying to digest the information I had just been given. Within minutes I heard the familiar sound of my dad's old truck rolling down our long gravel driveway. Still wet and shivering, I sprang to my feet and ran as fast as I could to the driveway and then into the street. The red tail lights were getting further and further away as I screamed for my parents to **_"STOP!"_** I screamed and cried aloud as my bare feet beat against the street, my heart pounding. In my twelve-year-old mind, I was certain that my parents were leaving/abandoning me. Why else would they tell me such a thing and then promptly take off?, I reasoned. I saw the white break lights go on in the darkness; our old green truck had stopped. I ran to the truck and as I reached the passenger door, it opened and my mother, who looked startled and concerned, couldn't get a word out before I cried out that I wanted to go with them and jumped inside the cab nearly knocking her over. It never felt so good to sit between my parents in my life.

I share this personal story because what happened to me is not unusual, perhaps the age at which I was told is out of the norm, but the feelings of fear, of no longer belonging, of not quite fitting in, of being a fifth wheel is not unique. Foremost, the fear of not being inherently enough or valued as much as biological children is a very powerful and imposing emotional terrain for any child to navigate. And that doesn't include the secondary shock and bewilderment that comes with the conscious or subconscious feelings of being valueless, not enough, and unworthy because one's own biological parent(s) did not want or keep you. Trust me, heroic stories of how selfless one's biological parent(s) may have been in giving you up do not matter or exist for a child; for a child it's all about *me* and why wasn't *'I'* good enough to be loved and wanted? Children do not possess the maturity or emotional/social insight necessary to appreciate that their biological parents may have been acting in their (the child's) best interests. It is a monumental task for a child to wrap their mind around all these facts and feelings, let alone understand them and manage to build a solid, healthy self identity and self esteem—they need help and support, and lots of it.

Good parents take care of this early on and use an array of loving and creative ways to re-enforce the fact that their adopted child was and is wanted by them, is equal to everyone else in the family, and in fact, holds a unique and special place in their hearts, a special place that no one else will ever possess. It is also a sacred trust and duty for the parent never to make the child wrong or require the child to meet some ancillary need the parent may have to be validated or honored because they adopted them. Considering the regular course of business for mothers as their children grow up, if a mother dumps that kind of toxic garbage on a child, then they're both in for a bumpy ride as the child tests boundaries and perhaps even punishes the offending parent for the emotional leveraging they were forced to endure as a result of being adopted *(or because they were/are step-children, foster children, etc.).*

What you must do

Tread lightly in this department and be sure never to hit below the belt. Don't say things that you can never take back. And likewise, if your child is insecure about their role in your family, then expect more testing in this department, but again, set your boundaries, don't allow yourself to become either a bully or a victim. Let your child know that you love and accept them and that your standard of love, care, acceptance, and expectation of respect is no different for them than it is for any other member of the family.

Beware too, that there are those rare occasions when an adopted child willfully decides to play the adoption card when they want something or as a means of controlling their parent(s) through guilt or self pity. Remember that they are your kid, period, and that you must not tolerate inappropriate or disrespectful behaviors from them just because they are adopted. And if you're dealing with this particular dynamic, do not placate them, give in to them, or make excuses for them. When adopted children are acting out in this way, they have taken on either the bully or the victim role as a means of acting-out or leveraging you. They may ultimately select you as their emotional punching bag as a means of exorcising the pain inside them via exacting some kind of cosmic revenge for being unwanted or adopted (i.e., acting out original abandonment). In most cases, conscientious parents do a great job of integrating the child's pre-adoption past early-on and creating an atmosphere of love and security for their family-of-choice. However, if you have lovingly set boundaries and diligently enforced them and the behavior continues or escalates, find a good therapist and go with your child to counseling.

When your adult child marries

A Son is a son until he takes a wife
A daughter is a daughter for the rest of your life!

Whether that's true for you or not, there does exist the phenomenon of in-law/outlaw feuds that emerge when a marriage occurs. The obvious challenge of blending families aside, it is amazing how often the mothers of the adult children getting married suddenly become not just mother-in-laws, but *Monster-in-laws*—and so they are portrayed in today's youth culture and pop media. But is it true? According to Samuel Butler everything changes when a son marries. The twentieth century Cambridge graduate, author, philosopher, and member of the clergy wrote: *"A man's friendships are like his will, invalidated by marriage—but they are also no less invalidated by the marriage of his friends."* Many a mother would argue that this extends to the grooms family as well.

So let's dive in. Maybe you have been labeled a monster-in-law and you're suffering deeply as a result. If so, take a deep breath, realize you're not alone, and remember, this book is written for us—the mothers. So keep your chin up and let's learn some things that may help us monster-in-laws understand why we're in the predicament we are and what we can do about it.

Although it is a widely accepted social condition that comedians poke fun at and we see portrayed as a situation to be pitied or laughed at in television and films, is our cultural view of mother-in-laws accurate? You don't hear much, if anything at all about father-in-law drama and there are no demeaning titles or euphemisms associated with them; therefore, we will stick to the title of our book and focus our attention on mothers, mothers who I believe, with a few rare exceptions, get a bum rap most of the time.

An interesting statistic

What's more common—the mother of the groom or the mother of the bride being labeled a *monster-in-law* and thereafter viewed as an interloper or enemy?

Answer:

I've asked countless men and women, husbands and wives, mothers and fathers, this question and hands down—it's the mother of the groom who is christened *Monster-in-law* more often than not. But I bet you knew that. So why do you think that's so?

First, remember what we know about boys and their emotional strengths and weaknesses, as well as their relationship with the alpha female in their lives. In general, what is the emotional constitution of your average groom? Remember, we're taking about the same boys who clung to their mammas and once they are committed to women, and then later to marriage, will give their wife the same love, trust, and allegiance they once gave to their mothers (as well they should). They will rely on their wives for all the emotional encouragement, support and strength they once got from their mothers. The transition is natural, logical, and predictable. But, at the end of the equation and at the end of the day, when the calculation is done—where once there was one alpha woman (mom), with the addition of a partner there is now potentially two alpha females in his life. Once married, there can only be one alpha female in a man's life, and it's *not* you, mom. That, I believe, is the rub for a lot of moms.

As Erich Fromm, the German-American, Jewish social psychologist, psychotherapist, and humanist so insightfully observed: *"The mother-child relationship is paradoxical and, in a sense, <u>tragic</u>. It requires the most intense love on the mother's side, yet this very love must help the child grow away from (her) the mother (the very source of that love) and to become fully independent."*

If you still don't get it. Here's a simple yet important mathematical equation for you to solve:

With what we know and admit to be true about the competitive and territorial nature of most women *(both the bride and the groom's mother) coupled with what we know about men—*

How many women, regardless of their title or status (or because of it) can a man

Give his heart to . . .
Rely upon . . .
Be there exclusively for . . .
Commit to entirely . . .

Take marching order from . . .
Perform honey-do chores for . . .
Spend the majority of his time with . . .
Be supportive of and supported by . . .

<u>Love exclusively and unconditionally with all his heart, mind, soul, and body forever</u>

C'mon, you know the answer!

What *(in most instances)* is the answer _____

(If your answer is one [1] congratulations, you get an "A")

In the case of the daughter-in-law dilemma, I am taking a leap of faith and assuming that you are not an abusive parent or mother-in-law and that you raised your children with love and have either authentically embraced their spouse/significant other, or you've put your best, most sincere foot forward and have sincerely tried with all your heart to accept your adult child's partner or spouse. If you've done all that and still you find yourself a stranger to your son and an unwelcome interloper to your daughter-in-law, please work hard to take-in the information given to you above and the information to follow. Also consider that now-a-days, both *people* and *love* itself have become commodities or possessions to many people. A territorial woman believes and behaves this way and will cling to and hoard her man just as tenaciously as the coveted designer purse she snatched off the clearance table, and she'll bear her teeth to protect and keep it. When two alpha females experience territorial challenges over a man who is both son and husband, often times the math just doesn't work out for mom. *★The same alpha female dynamics often come into play when a father with daughters remarries*

What about son-in-laws?

My research has not indicated that there's a big problem looming with men relative to their mother-in-law. Perhaps between the two respective mother-in-laws, yes, there can definitely be competitive issues, but by and large, men/husbands simply want to duck and cover when it comes to this kind of emotional territoriality and warfare. Furthermore, (pay attention to this mom) men will almost without exception seek the path of least resistance and drama relative to the person with whom they share their lives, and again, that's not you mom. Maybe that's why the bible says that a man "*shall leave* (what?)—*his mother* and *cleave* to **his wife**." Maybe it's just the way we women are wired. Whatever the cause, more times than not, when it comes to mother-in-law issues, they exist almost exclusively between wives and their mother-in-laws. The alpha female factor and strict territoriality creates an atmosphere ripe with conflict and drama that is either overt and palatable, or lying just under the surface. There are a million other little things that can factor in, but after interviewing dozens of mothers, at the end of the day, it all boils down to simple alpha female competition and dominance; after all, how many adult/mature female birds have you seen living in one nest?

So what's a mother to do?

It's short and it's sweet. If you're verbally, emotionally, or god forbid physically abused, neglected or abandoned, then set appropriate boundaries; and after you've done that-get yourself a life, and by that, I mean *a life of your own.*

If you've been a good mom and lived your life entirely for your children, I know those are harsh words to hear, and if, like me, being a *mother* was your entire identity, then being on the outside looking in, perhaps from afar, has been a completely devastating event for you. Beyond that, it may very well have ushered in unprecedented emotions and behaviors. Behaviors that hold the potential of deeply harming you; things like: isolation, depression, and/or self medication—all results of you being *at the affect* of the mathematical equation we mentioned earlier rather than deciding to learn some new math for yourself and your life. Remember, it's never too late to be *at cause* in the matter of your life rather than always being at the affect of the actions or inactions of those around you. We'll talk more about what we can do to improve our self esteem and quality of life later. For now, we want to identify the relationships that are hurting you and attempt an explanation that does not include making yourself a bad mother, wrong, cursed, or at fault for the current state of affairs.

If you are still not convinced that it is YOU that must change . . .

Without a doubt, there are times when a well-meaning son or daughter-in-law encounters the *mother-in-law from hell*, but again, that is not the mother who this book is written for. If you are such a mother, then examine the mathematical equation referenced in this chapter and realize that your adult child is grown and must now 'do life' on their own and with a mate of their own. You are no longer their immediate caregiver, teacher or guardian, not even if you want to be; it's *not* your job anymore, so let them go! Give your adult child/children the gift of independence. Allow them to make their own mistakes in life—release them.

If you consider yourself a good mother who did the best she could, and whether it's your son, your daughter, your son-in-law, or your daughter-in-law, I suspect that you have a well-rehearsed chorus of reasons and rationales for why you feel the way you do. You may have at the ready, all the facts, history, reasons and rationales that prove that you are 99.999% correct, and still, it does not change the fact that you're in an incredible amount of pain. Nor does it change the stone cold fact that being *'right'* will not bring you the love and connection you desire. Some of you will die insisting that you're right, while there are others of you, and I'd guess it's the majority of you who have done the opposite—you have blamed yourself.

Rhonda's Story . . . .

Rhonda's son was her pride and joy. There was no father on the scene, yet, in spite of the challenges, Rhonda was determined to raise her four children alone, and that she did. The family was poor but always had clean clothes, food, a roof over their heads and attended church every Sunday. Rhonda is representative of single mothers all over the country who valiantly work full-time while raising their children on their own, often with no assistance from the children's father.

Rhonda thought she was experiencing the typical challenges parents of teenagers encounter and was also quick to admit that she self-medicated after a long day at work by enjoying a few beers to ease her nerves; a practice her older son Mitchell was very critical of. Her son left home immediately after graduating high school and married shortly thereafter. Prior to meeting his future wife, Rhonda's son stayed in touch with his mother, grandmother, and siblings on a regular basis, but once he married, all contact with his family abruptly stopped. Rhonda was devastated and wondered what she had done wrong. Attempts to reconcile with her estranged son erupted into bitter battles with her new daughter-in-law. Rhonda admitted that when the sparks started flying, she *gave as good as she got*. She also admitted to secretly hoping that the marriage would fail. As time passed, Rhonda tried to make peace. She waited and prayed, and intermittently she attempted contact with them.

Fifteen years later, Rhonda still waits! She has not seen her son in all those years, nor has she ever laid eyes on her grandchild. Rhonda lives life with a hole in her heart that at times, especially around the holidays or her birthday, feels like a bottomless pit that threatens to swallow her up. Her other children don't understand why their brother, the one they looked up to, vanished from their lives. Rhonda is comforted by the fact that she does have her other children, as well as a deep and abiding faith that God watches over her. Those connections and her deep spiritual faith help Rhonda through many a dark and lonely night. Sadly, I would learn that Rhonda's story is not unique.

What kind of mother or mother-in-law are you?

Where mother-in-laws have been historically stereotyped and labeled the villain and a new wife's arch-nemesis in literature, cinema and pop culture, the truth is—it's a 50/50 proposition at best when it comes to creating drama and exercising the territoriality over the man in the middle. There are plenty of wonderful, loving, well-intended mother-in-laws who simply (via their having given birth to their sons) have become nothing more than an intrusion and unwelcome interloper in the eyes of their daughter-in-law. They are seen as an obstacle to absolute control over both their husbands and their new life. In fact, my research and interviews have revealed an interesting statistical fact: mothers who enjoyed close and friendly relationships with their sons, are usually the first to get the proverbial kick in the kiester when the new wife moves in because they're viewed as competition for the new bride's attention. In the end, it cuts both way. The days of the mother of the groom being blamed for all problems related to a daughter-in-law's unhappiness are gone. Don't own that! For every Monster-in-law (and they do exist) there most certainly are Devilish Daughter-in-laws, and some of you know this firsthand.

How many of you moms have been the first one to extend the olive branch or a hug, to apologize for something you did not do, take responsibility for another person's emotional condition and again apologize and try to fix it, only to be hurt again. Have you knowingly and politely tolerated knives in the back and still smiled, still gave of yourself, still loved unconditionally, still hoped for the best? Is that you? Have you ever wondered *why* you keep doing it? It's because you're a mother. It's how you're hardwired and what you're made for. From the moment of conception, there existed between you and your child, a bond, a mental, emotional, spiritual, and physical bond. The physical manifestation of that bond (the umbilical cord) was cut at birth, but in a very real way, we mothers remain tethered to our children for better or worse. We mothers are conditioned from the moment of our child's birth to love and be there for them no matter what, even when they hurt us. So please, don't beat yourself up. Instead, I want you to take a moment and accept a sincere *thank you* for the job you've done, and then, pat yourself on the back for being the mother you've been and continue to be.

What we shared thus far may or may not resonate with you. Not all families function or dys-function in this way, but certainly the majority of families I encountered share many common expectations and experiences. If you have no idea what I'm talking about or have never experienced any of the situations, emotions, disappointments or conditions described thus far, then you are among the lucky few who have escaped parenthood, marriage, and in-law-hood unscathed. We envy and celebrate you.

CHAPTER 5

All in the Family—Part II

Step-parenting & the Blended Family

Step-parenting

Here is an eye opener—while the divorce rate among couples married for the first time is somewhere between 50-55%, it is even higher (with some estimates placing it between 60-70%) among marriages that include step-children. The entire process of divorce, remarriage and step-parenting is one that must be thoroughly understood before exposing oneself, a significant other and children to the challenging reality of blending families.

How divorce and remarriage can affect children

Children of divorce must cope with having their parent's marriage broken apart and with them not only living in separate houses but often engaged in all-out warfare. These children struggle to find balance and attempt to maintain healthy relations with each of their parents. If a new boyfriend/girlfriend are instantly thrown into that mix, and marriage or living-together follows, that can really send younger children into a tailspin as they face the mammoth challenge of learning to co-exist inside a new lifestyle with an entirely new set of expectations.

With one out of two first-time marriages ending in divorce, step-families are becoming increasingly more common in this country as divorced men and women with children give marriage another try. Unfortunately, as the number of step-families increase, so does the divorce rate. The complicated structure and cross-culture dynamics inherent in such families puts an extra stress on the marriage and all its constituents.

If living together inside the agreement of marriage is challenging, and raising children is even more challenging because it's a life-time commitment that a parent cannot (or should not) walk away from, then living with or relating to step-children/step-parents is an outright uphill battle for most parties attempting to blend families. An overwhelming majority of the divorced parents interviewed for this book identified issues involving step-children and/or their husband or wife's ex-spouse as the primary source of stress and conflict in the marriage and the chief reason for marriage problems. It also explains why the divorce rate for remarried couples with children is substantially higher for blended families than for first-time marriages or a second or third marriage that does not include children.

How divorce and remarriage can affect a step-parent—or—Why step-parenting can be so difficult

First, let me again clarify that this book is written for *parents* not children, in particular: *mothers;* therefore, our primary focus will be on the role and experiences of step-mothers as opposed to step-children.

There are stepmothers who enjoy a pleasant and supportive relationship with their stepchild from day one; however, anecdotally, in my research experience that's rare. More prevalent is a situation where both parties (step-parent and stepchild) feel suspicious and uncertain about an ancillary relationship they did not chose and may feel is being forced upon them. Children are especially prone to feeling this way and can be terribly cruel in their treatment of their mother or father's new partner. Adults who behave this way toward their step-children, particularly young/minor children should have considered their role and what the challenges would be *before* getting involved with a single parent. After all, they are the adult and have a higher duty of care to fulfill.

When your stepchildren are adults

When the step-child involved is an adult, and if they behave badly, the same rules regarding inappropriate or disrespectful behavior that apply to one's own children apply to them but with a twist. In the case of step-children, the boundaries and behavioral expectation must be made clear from the on-set of the relationship and it is the adult stepchild's parent that *must* lay down the law and oversee its consistent enforcement. The reason for this is that many step-parents are either openly viewed as interlopers and consequently are discarded and disrespected or they are perceived as having no power and certainly no right to offer input or establish rules or boundaries regarding their step-child's behavior. When that is the case, it is both frustrating and futile to assert one's point of view or communicate expectations that will only serve as fodder for the fire—that is why it is their parent's duty to set standards and establish healthy boundaries and expectations surrounding their child's behavior. When I consider what we know to be true about E-generation kids, my heart goes out to that segment of caring, well-meaning step-parents who are met with disrespect, rejection, territoriality, hostility, subterfuge, and often, outright attempts to undermine their role and perhaps even the marriage itself. Sadly, for women entering a relationship where these specific dynamics exist, being a stepmother is without a doubt, a daunting, tumultuous, and often times, thankless call to duty to their new family.

Many optimistic step-parents enter a new family expecting to share love and quickly build close bonds of trust and affection with their stepchildren and become confused and deflated when their efforts are not well-received or not received at all. It is like flipping a coin and waiting to see how it lands when it comes to a stepchild's response to a new partner or spouse. Some experts claim that it can take up to seven years for certain children to adjust to a step-parent. Good Lord, that's longer than the average blended marriage these days, and no wonder! For children who are openly hostile towards a step-parent, they may feel deep loyalties to their parents even if those parents hate each other and are dysfunctional, or they may possess a sense of ownership of their parent and view their parent's new partner as an unwelcome interloper.

Karen's story

Karen experienced both sides of the stepmother coin toss. She married Mark, a man with two daughters. Herself having two children, Karen appreciated the fact that there would be diligent work involved in successfully blending their families. She had always been very conscientious and responsible when it came to modeling/ teaching her own children that respect for others was an absolute. When she and Mark married, no challenges were made to his entry or position in the family and comfortable relationships between him and his new stepchildren soon formed; Mark's daughters were another story entirely.

Karen anticipated having a tough go-of-it with Mark's youngest daughter from his second marriage. The child was very close to her mother and intensely loyal. She had also been used as both leverage and an emotional weapon by her mother since her parent's divorce, with the result being that her relationship with her father was precarious at best. Karen reasoned that she would more than likely be viewed as an intruder and just another adult to be skeptical of and mistrust, optimistically determined, she was ready to take on the challenge. Karen's concern and attention was so focused on developing and nurturing a relationship with her new husband's youngest daughter that she didn't give much thought to what lay ahead of her with his oldest. After all, Karen told herself, her kids were adults and had readily accepted Mark, so what possible problem could arise with Mark's adult daughter from his first marriage? She was away at college and wouldn't be living with them, so how challenging could creating a healthy connection with her be? In defiance of all her expectations, Mark's youngest daughter embraced her with open arms and an open heart and the relationship flourished. His oldest daughter was an entirely different story. Karen related that both she and her marriage to the young woman's father were met with open hostility and flagrant attempts to create conflict, competition, and disruption of both the marriage and budding family unit.

Given what we know about some of the less than flattering female personality constructs and mother/daughter (female on female) dynamics, it is no wonder that an E-generation female adult daughter would challenge the new woman on the scene who she sees an the enemy invader of *her territory*. Karen reported that the behaviors ranged from bizarre to belligerent and were extremely destructive at times, so much so, that the stress and division created as a result of challenging Karen's entry into Mark's life nearly destroyed the marriage. Fortunately, the couple got into therapy, and although it was difficult and initially inflamed the situation even more, they were able to establish behavioral mandates and boundaries around what was *acceptable* and *unacceptable* behavior, and stick to it.

Will your role as step-mother result in a step-up or a step-on experience?

With an estimated divorce rate of approximately 60-70% among step-families, it would be unfair and untrue to tell you that you don't have your work cut out for you. And we've only scratched the surface of step-parent/stepchild relations. We haven't even touched on the complicated and messy challenges that step-parents encounter with their husband or wife's ex-spouse and how that can negatively impact and affect the stability of their marriage.

Turf Wars

I cannot tell you emphatically enough how important it is that step-children be keenly made aware of what I call **The Rules of the Road** when a new spouse takes up residence in your home, or when you move into your new spouse's home; a home which has been occupied by children who, no matter their age, will feel very intruded upon and are likely to rather adamantly inform you that it's *'their house.'* Nothing can make the adjustment to a new marriage and a blended family more abysmal than trying to accomplish that challenging feat in an environment where you feel like an outsider and the kids are predisposed to feeling territorial about their habitat. While composing this book, I've heard horror stories of new husbands and wives who were told by their step-children that the family home was not their house and that they (the kids) did not have to listen to the step-parent, keep rooms clean, wash dishes, sweep the floor, dust, etc. or do anything the new step-parent asked the child to do. Virtually every parent I interviewed expressed feeling uncomfortable to one degree or another when moving into an established home. They felt this way either because their new spouse had lived in the home with his or her ex or because their step-children openly made them feel unwelcome or inferior, in that they felt they had no say about their shared home because it was not viewed as being theirs too. Of course, in a perfect world, where money, schools, and the rigors and expense of moving are not a consideration, it is always best to start off a second/third marriage in a new home that, although shared with the children, belongs to the adults, and the kids know this! Because that is usually not feasible, that makes it all the more important that children be told in no uncertain terms that this new person in their life is mommy or daddy's best friend and life partner, and that because of that, the house they once shared alone, now belongs to the adults but will be lovingly and respectfully shared by everyone. Children must know that after marriage and upon moving in, the step-parent entering the home is imbued with all the rights and privileges of ownership and that the children *must* acknowledge and respect that.

Marriage—Kids—and the Ex Factor

Short and sweet: children of divorce often resent the new step-parent and resist the idea of them entering the family. They often express a sense of being disloyal to their mother if they're accepting of their new step-mother, or conversely, they may feel they're being disloyal to their father if they're accepting of, or nice to their new step-father. The web of drama can be endless and emotionally exhausting to navigate, and many times, children, parents, and step-parents alike get lost in it. Ex-spouses can make powerful enemies of a new spouse, particularly if they're insecure and jealous of their relationship with their former spouse and with their child. Children do suffer the most in scenarios like this. And saddest of all, most of the drama unfolding around the step-parent is completely out of their control. That is why it takes a person of strong perseverance and determination to succeed at creating a balanced, high-functioning, and happy step-family. All in all, to take on all these challenges and the intimidating statistics of failure surrounding them, is no small feat. The best advice is to:

- ❖ Seek a clear and honest understanding of all the relationship dynamics that exist for *all* parties involved *before* jumping in
- ❖ Get into a healthy counseling environment where each person can be heard and have their feelings and concerns validated and addressed
- ❖ Assure your children of your love for them and create special times and rituals with them to share with you, but . . .
- ❖ Put your coupleship first
- ❖ Set healthy boundaries and establish realistic expectations and goals
- ❖ Maintain those standards for yourself and for your children and stepchildren
- ❖ Find a balance between forgiveness and second chances and respect for yourself, your boundaries, and your own emotional health and sanctity
- ❖ Be willing to do the work and be patient
- ❖ When you've done this—start at the top of the list and repeat the process again if necessary.
- ❖ Marriage, like any meaningful relationship is not a 50/50 proposition—it's a 100/100 proposition. Each partner must give not just half of what they can but ALL of what they have to their coupleship and the creation of a healthy family unit. But, if you know in your heart of hearts that you've given 100%, exhausted all measures, and yet, you cannot make the blended family work, then it's time to know where you are and what you want from life.

CHAPTER 6

Driving in Cars with Children!
Who's Driving Your Car?

We have talked about what our culture called the MTV generation/ Generation X and the radical shift that took place in the traditional family structure of our country via what I identify as *the E-generation;* and although we touched on this subject earlier, it warrants more scrutiny and understanding because good or bad, baby-boomers, for the most part, grew up with a solid family identity, a sense of national pride as children, and a keen sense of where they fit into the scheme of things.

Boomers and the children born before them, grew up waving the flag, singing the National Anthem proudly, and declaring the Pledge of Allegiance each morning in school. They were also taught to respect their parents and authority figures, in fact, it was practically branded into their hind ends as children, both metaphorically and for some of us, physically as well. Later, with the new era of technology, came major cultural upheaval; the old, established institutions were challenged and rebelled against, and the fallout from all that, was a generation of kids who raised themselves and whose role models were MTV, video games like Nintendo, and who many times, came from a dysfunctional or broken home. These same kids found solace in their video games, mp3 players, and eventually the internet. Generation X and the E-generation not only followed in the footsteps of the hippie generation in challenging their parents, they were encouraged to by social institutions, institutions that would abandon the Ten Commandments, the National Anthem and even the Pledge of Allegiance. The E-generation was the first generation of American children to be exposed to disturbing levels of violence on television and in the movies. When boomers were kids, it was a safe bet that if the bad guy got shot in a movie and definitely on television, there was no blood and gore visible; everything was sanitized when we were kids. Today, many frustrated and confused E-generation kids have grown up lacking a moral compass or family structure; that, along with the progression of violence in films and video games in our society came the horror of school and workplace shootings, a social nightmare that is most predominant in America; and is it any wonder? The gore and violence that has infiltrated and proliferated in the American media since the 80's is an indictment of our society and its lack of morality and standards. It's tragically shocking that during the course of a few generations, a total collapse of family structure occurred. The disappearance of solid role models and reliable family and societal structure, and in its place came an age of reckless abandon in which E-generation kids exercised their authority and expressed themselves in ways never seen before.

On a much less tragic scale, the exercise of will and rebellious independence by teenagers and young adults can be seen in the ways they express themselves via what they call 'body art.' I recalled a time when for days my generally outspoken, extroverted teenager didn't have a single comment or compliant, never spoke back, and over-all, had no opinion whatsoever to express. I found it highly unusual, that is, until I later discovered that he had secretly had his tongue pierced and didn't want me to see the large stud in the center of his tongue. It never occurred to him that he should ask for permission, nor did it occur to the tattoo parlor he visited that they should ask to see identification to insure that he was legally of age. How many parents can identify with this? Your minor child (usually a teenager) has come home with a tattoo or a piercing that you did not authorize? Or they threaten to get one if you don't comply with some adolescent mandate, as we will see in Simon's story. This is the same emotional bullying and blackmail that takes place when the school yard bully threatens to punch the puny kid if they don't give up their lunch money, except in this scenario—you're the puny kid.

Simon's Story

Simon had only one child, a daughter who he loved dearly and admittedly spoiled rotten. While on spring break, Simon's daughter quickly ran threw all her allotted money and available credit as kids are prone to do. Still having days left to party, she immediately called dad demanding more cash. The young woman went through all the ploys in the princess play book but when they didn't work, being short on patience and insistent in her demands for more money Simon's daughter became angry and indignant. As Simon's daughter grew more and more infuriated by her father's hesitancy to comply, it suddenly dawned on Simon that in his daughter's reality, the world was *her kingdom* and he was merely one of her subjects, thereby mandating that both his allegiance and money rightfully belonged to her. As this light began to dawn on Simon, he became stronger and remained surprisingly loving but stalwart in his resolve not to give his spoiled daughter any more money. When demanding did not work, Simon's daughter switched gears and went back into crying, pouting, and manipulating mode. For the first time in his life Simon held his ground (but only by a mere thread of will power). The notion of not getting whatever she wanted from dad was foreign to Simon's daughter, so in response to his aberrant behavior she cranked up the volume and took the game to the next level—she began screaming at him. Finally, the drama concluded with this very manipulative E-generation woman/child threatening her father with a tattoo if he did not wire money to her immediately. Yes, you read it right, the young woman in this story held her own body for ransom in order to extort money from her very-conservative Jewish father. The fate of this poor father's only daughter's body and maintaining its sanctity now lay in the balance. It was a strategic move on her part; she knew what would bother her father most—a tattoo!

Note: tattooing is not an acceptable practice for conservative Jews, in fact, if tattooed, a member cannot be buried in a conservative Jewish cemetery, so you can imagine dad's upset and concern—Oy Vey!

How is this behavior any different than that of the well cared for, deeply loved, child who comes home from school and begins dictating to his or her parents? In my opinion, as well as in the opinions and experiences of the parents whose stories are told throughout this book, there is no difference. It's the same learned tactic played out over and over again against unsuspecting, unprepared parents. The teenage girl who demanded a car from her mother used the same behavior but in her case, she ramped up the behavior and escalated her demands and insistence on getting her way to such a level that she resorted to violence in order to insure that she maintained dominance and control.

By the way, in Simon's case, his daughter's ploy backfired on her. She over-reached in her attempt to manipulate and control her father, and by doing so, only managed to make him more steadfast in his resolve. When Simon was able to objectively identify the depths of her manipulation and the lengths to which she would go to extract money from him, he took a deep breath and for the first time in his relationship with his daughter, he said *"no"* and meant it. Emotionally bruised and battered but determined, Simon warned his daughter that if she showed up back at school with a tattoo, he'd cut her off, and with that retort, he calmly hung up the phone while the sounds of his only daughter screaming her lungs out on the other end of the line fizzled away in the background. Score one for dad!

Raising Kids is like driving a car down life's highway

As parents there are two very basic rules of the road that are plain and clear at the beginning, or at least should be plain, clear, and practiced at the onset and throughout this ride we take in life called *parenting*. If parenting is the car, then we must remember that—*1) we own the car—2) We hold the keys and—3) we drive the car.*

When points one through three are clear, that also implies that we decide where the car is going and what its final destination is; however, sadly many of us parents gave up the keys either willingly or the car was hijacked by our children a long time ago. And if we've surrendered the keys, it's no wonder we have suffered and continue to, it's because we surrendered our role as DRIVER/ PARENT a long time ago. We are no longer in control. We gave up the reins, and for some of us, we're not even in the passenger seat; we've been relegated to the backset, and in some cases, the trunk. Parents who get thrown into the trunk are the ones who made too much noise or caused too much grief for their children by objecting to, or forbidding certain behaviors or privileges. But their child does still love them and they definitely need their parent from time to time, and in those instances the child driver will pull their parent out of the trunk, dust them off, and plunk the thankful parent into the back seat every now and then or on a *need-to* basis. For those of you looking for the trunk to open up or for a ray of sunshine to appear through a crack, the only consoling news is there is a fate worse than yours. If a parent is viewed as an obstacle to a free life or is simply a pain in the ass to their adult child, they get tossed out onto the highway. Once that happens, not only are you no longer in the car with your child, you're out on a desolate stretch of road, alone, bewildered, and wondering how this could happen to you.

I've been in all conceivable locations in the car, and I've been tossed out and left alone, abandoned on a lonely highway we call *'Life without your child's love, approval, acceptance or respect.'* It is a place where you feel empty, deserted, scared, and alone. You may be walking down that long lonely highway now, asking yourself what you did wrong. It is both sad and ironically funny how, once booted out onto the highway, you begin to think that maybe the trunk wasn't so bad after all; at least, *in the trunk,* you were in your child's life. And then, you do what so many mothers (and some fathers do) you rationalize that if you just don't rock the boat so much, don't upset them so much, just go with the flow, then you could probably make your way back into the trunk or maybe even into the coveted backseat of what was once *your car.* For now, let's keep walking together because I promise, there is ray of light at the end of the road. Incidentally, just in case anyone is asking—how do you go from the driver's seat, to the passenger seat, to the back seat, the trunk, and then ultimately are strewn along the highway? The answers given by the parents I met along the highway were simple and seem to be somewhat unified. If you think about it and honestly analyze your behavior, you'll no doubt agree that we all know when and to whom we surrendered both the keys and the driver's seat. Perhaps you are still in the passenger seat, sitting quietly and approvingly, or trying to be *hip or cool* as you proudly wear the name tag labeled *'friend;'* and maybe you're fine there. Just beware that your seat, whether passenger or backseat, may be given away to another *'friend'* if you stop meeting needs or begin to behave like a *parent* rather than a contemporary vying to maintain a *friendship* with them. Remember, your child has only one mother, but if you've abandoned that role in order to become a friend, beware—they have lots of friends, so as one of many, you are now a replaceable commodity.

So let's take a closer look at the vehicle we call parenthood; let's examine seat assignments. There's the front, the back, and then there is . . . the trunk! The trunk is reserved for parents who behaved badly and/or parents who tried to take the keys back a time or two. Nothing teaches a pesky parent better than putting you in the trunk for a while; it sucks to be in the dark, doesn't it? By now you know the rules and if you play by them and stop rocking the boat (or the car), you may earn your way back into the backseat or even into the passenger seat, but the driver's seat? No way! You gave that up a long time ago baby. And how about those unfortunate few who get tossed altogether? Again, this pre-supposes that you embodied the role of parent fairly, lovingly and diligently. If you did all this, and still you've been left behind, abandoned, tossed to the wind—why is that? Why did it happen to you, a good mother? Why, why, why? You cry. In my experience, as well as in the experiences of other well-meaning parents, there is a simple answer to this heart-rending question. When you gave up that driver's seat a long time ago, settling for the passenger seat, then the back seat, and were then relegated to the trunk, before getting the final boot, one or two things usually occur. The first is easy to identify—you got tossed from the trunk the minute you decided that you've had enough, that it is high time to take the driver's seat back. You put your parent boots back on and attempted to draw a line in the sand for that self-empowered, self-indulged E-generation child of yours, and they (now accustomed to having all the power) handily rejected your challenge. A warning must be heralded to all parents who decide that they're mad as hell and they're not going to take it anymore.

WARNING—attempting to resume a position of authority and/or demanding respect, when none has been given in the past and when you've settled for *less than* that for years, is more than enough incentive for an immature, unenlightened, unappreciative child to give you the boot, and usually, depending on the level of their entitlement and sense of empowerment, it can happen rapidly and with harsh disregard or slowly and subtly. Either way, the message is clear—*Hit the road Jack!*

Remember the woman who told her daughter (the honor roll student) that she couldn't have the luxury sports car she demanded? That mother was pistol-whipped and had her very life threatened when she attempted to put her parent boots back on. Makes that lonely stretch of desolate highway not seem quite so bad, doesn't it? And now you know it's not so lonely after all, you have fellow parents traveling that same stretch of highway.

Parental note: the reason I call them parent boots is because it is almost a certainty that you're already knee-deep in %&@# and that you're going to have to wade through a considerable amount of it in order to get your life and your relationship cleaned up, focused, and back on track again. You might also have to give the driver of that car of yours, what my father used to call a *'swift kick in the ass'* and there's nothing more fitting than boots for that particular chore. Of course, I am speaking proverbially and not physically.

And while we're talking about *retaking the hill*, or *the car* in our metaphor, and the likely negative response to your efforts, words of simple honesty, intelligent insight, and practical wisdom come to mind. Appropriately, they are the words of a great American

General who warned us that **being responsible and doing the right thing sometimes means pissing people off.** Bear these realities in mind when you decide to put your parent boots back on.

The Second catalyst for being tossed occurs when your adult–child or teen, aligns themselves with a peer group or significant other that has virtually no respect for the role of parent or other authority figures. This new peer or significant other may also have tossed one or both of their parents out of their life as well. In many cases, the peer group or significant other has no specific agenda with the parents but simply wishes to exercise complete dominance, influence, and control over the subject of their interest, in this case, it just happens to be your son or daughter. Men who are not allowed to maintain contact with former friends (both male and female) once they become involved with a new/possessive woman fall into this category. Incidentally, virtually every parent or former friend who has experienced this type of social ostracism reported that without exception, their adult–child or friend went willingly; that speaks to how powerful and influential these relationships can be.

Beverly's story

Beverly's 18 year old son married right out of high school and with the nuptials came a battle royal. You see, both the new bride and the groom's mother had a tenacious, almost fanatical sense of ownership of this young man. Their individual sense of territoriality brought with it plenty of tension and drama, as well as awe and destruction. Beverly admits that she and her son were close and that because of his young age, she was not supportive of the impromptu teen-marriage but emphatically states that she did give the appearance of joy and support for her son's sake. I'm sure many mothers out there can relate to this tale. How many of you have 'faked it' for the sake of your child, thinking you were putting on a stellar performance when in reality, your true feelings were more than likely very transparent. If so, you probably know how Beverly's story ended. If not, let me share. As time went by and no annulment or divorce was announced, Beverly changed gears and made several attempts to reconcile with her son and new daughter-in-law but no ground was given up by the offended young wife. The couple changed their number and moved away. The young bride made no bones about making her husband choose between her and his mother; there would be no peace treaty, no easing of strained relations, no détente', no-nothin'! Beverly was on the highway, tossed out and alone. Over the years, the young couple had their ups and downs and even came dangerously close to divorce a time or two, but they stuck it out and remained together. Beverly extended olive branches whenever she could but they were all rejected.

If you don't *'get'* how powerful (and disempowering) giving up the driver's seat when your children are young is, or how settling for the passenger seat effects your relationship with your child forever, get it now! In spite of her faith, prayers, and multiple efforts, Beverly was never able to shift things back. During the first year of marriage, Beverly and the young man's wife waged terrific battles but the young bride won the war, with the result being that Beverly lost all contact with her son. A decade later, she and her son are still estranged, and although she now has four beautiful grandchildren, Beverly has never heard their voices or laid eyes on them. Please note that I intentionally used the words 'battle' and 'war' to describe the dynamics between these two women (mother and daughter-in-law) because sadly, they apply in this scenario; however, these descriptions are not healthy/holistic terms and should never be desired or haphazardly used to describe intra-family relations. The truth we can take from Beverly's situation and from the dozens and dozens of families living under a declaration of war, is that—

Love can be many things, but what it is not, and must never be is:

Tested *as if it were an exam you are giving to the other person*

Treated as Property *where it is lorded over or treated as territory you alone own and control*

Waged as a war *where other sources of love are not welcome but rather are suspiciously viewed as a competitor to be destroyed or where there must be a winner and a loser.*

Begin to assimilate and embody this simple yet profound truth

Love cannot be owned, only given freely from an open heart and then nurtured, cherished and given away again, and again, and again . . .

CHAPTER 7

Are You Acting as an Enabler to Your Own Abuse?

Take it from a former enabler and sufferer—it may be a hard pill to swallow but you may be acting as an enabler in your own worst nightmare.

We are all familiar with the terms *codependent* and *enabler* as it relates to alcoholics but usually don't consider ourselves codependent or enablers when we continue to tolerate the unacceptable behavior of our children or when we find ourselves constantly rescuing our adult children. When we engage in these behaviors, we *'good moms'* call it *love*, but is it really love or is it something else? Could part of it be loneliness, low self esteem or neediness on your part?

When our children are young, they have no choice in the matter as we basically own them and their lives (for want of a better, more politically correct term); whether they are good, bad, rebellious or disrespectful, we love and adore them, feed them, clothe them and provide a home for them. When our children become teens and grown into adulthood, we are supposed to teach them the practical and moral skills necessary to be a productive and responsible member of society and then relinquish our control by gradually handing the reins over to them. Unfortunately, in many instances, rather than a healthy transition taking place, a codependent relationship develops and ultimately leads to various kinds of leveraging and/or abuse. This happens when an E-generation adult child with an oversized sense of empowerment and entitlement still wants you to *do/provide/ serve* him or her and you're happy to do it in order to maintain control or stay in close emotional proximity to your child. Often times, when we define ourselves solely as a mother, we experience empty nest syndrome when our children grow up and move away either emotionally/socially or geographically. When this occurs, we are at risk of becoming vacant and needy. This happens because the solitary role/identity we had established for ourselves has either been challenged or vacated altogether and we no longer feel needed. Therefore, in order to keep our identity intact and continue to feel loved, needed, and validated we are more than happy to play the role of fixer, pleaser, server, rescuer, and in some cases, slave to our adult children. Furthermore, there is an inherent pay-off in this kind of relationship for both parties. Your adult child gets their material needs met and doesn't have to assume full responsibility for their life or actions, and you feel temporarily needed and valued. Everyone is happy, but only for a short while because even you know when you're being used. Most of the mothers I have spoken with said they went from server/rescuer to indentured servant, and a few described themselves as having graduated to *slave* to their adult child. Those that described themselves as slaves to their children also described themselves as victims in global terms, an interesting correlation. A word to those mothers: salves don't have a choice, and there are no victims—only volunteers.

When the tables get turned and you find yourself living to serve or rescue your child, the relationship dynamics have changed dramatically. The teen or adult child in your life is now officially in the driver's seat, and you, well you are going along for the ride hoping that a crumb of attention falls your way. This kind of relationship is not sustainable and will eventually implode. I know this only because I have firsthand experience with trying to win *value* and *approval* by constantly *doing* for my child. Oddly, the needier I became, the more I selflessly gave of myself, and the less I was respected both by my children and ultimately, by myself.

Samuel's Story

I have a friend whose daughter had been at odds with him since she was a young child. Divorced when she was ten years old, my friend Samuel was made out to be the *'bad guy'* in the divorce. The children were emotionally coached to mistrust him and to respond negatively to his attempts to maintain a bond with them. Visits with their father were strongly discouraged and severely judged when they occurred. Samuel's son, Peter refused to participate in this ostracism and continued to see his dad, while his daughter, wanting to please her mother, took sides, and repeatedly told her father that she hated him and did not want to see him again. Samuel would implore her, beg her, cry, and even attempted to bribe her; her only response was to denounce her father and throw colossal tantrums, refusing to go with him.

Finally, deflated and feeling completely defeated and estranged, Samuel quit asking. The young girl was no longer getting the attention she once did from her father and this infuriated her even more. You see, although the child was an innocent pawn being used by her mother to wage war against her father, on the surface, Samuel deprived her of an emotional punching bag and that made both mother and daughter resent him all the more. In addition to that, the young girl grew to loathe her brother for his *"betrayal"* of their mother. The infrastructure of this family was utterly destroyed because one party (the mother) had to assuage her feelings of anger and resentment by turning her children into weapons to use against her ex-husband/their own father; the collateral damage was horrific. The goal of using her children as pawns in the divorce worked successfully with regard to her daughter but had tragic results with her son, who bonded deeply with his father and grew more and more estranged from his mother and sister who both viewed and treated him as if he were a traitor. The mistrust, rivalry, and acrimony swelled like a raging sea until Peter's (once adoring) little sister grew to despise him as much as she did her father. Samuel's son felt a combination of contempt and pity for his bitter mother and sister. Sadly, this family, its relationships and the innocence of two children were sacrificed at the altar of ego and revenge.

The years passed and my friend Samuel, continued to see his son; their relationship blossomed and enriched both their lives, and although he loved his daughter, her animosity was so great for him that he simply became numb to the pain of her absence in his life. As time passed, Samuel's daughter watched as her father's car rolled into their driveway every other Friday night, picked up her brother and then drove away into the night. And so it was for years.

It was an unexpected call that brought Samuel's daughter back into his life. Ten years of total estrangement had passed. She was twenty, living with, and fiercely fighting with her mother and now wanted out. She also wanted a car. Samuel immediately saw a need he could meet and thought that perhaps that would put him in good standing with his estranged daughter. He drove to his ex-wife's house, picked up his daughter and her belongings, rented her an apartment and then bought her a car. She did not say thank you but rather behaved as if he owed it to her. Samuel did not utter a word of objection regarding her lack of manners or gratitude, as Samuel's own guilt would not allow him to address the disrespectful way she treated him, instead, he allowed it because as he would later tell me: *"at least I had contact with her again and she wasn't screaming at me."*

As the years and decades passed, Samuel retired and moved to another state. His son remained in constant contact and always implored his father to move back because he missed him. His daughter stayed in contact too, but it was never a gratifying or enriching experience for either one of them. His daughter would call to remind him of the many ways he had let her down over the years or to expound on what an awful father he had been. She also called to check up on what he (Samuel) had done for her brother but not for her. The rivalry was still firmly intact. For Samuel, it was a constant emotional and financial siege. What he thought would be a reconciliatory relationship when he brought his daughter back into his life had become an exercise in torment for my friend. It was as if he owed a debt that he could never repay.

All the years I knew Samuel as a neighbor, he was a bright, creative, happy, and delightfully funny ray of light in the lives of those who knew him. The only dark and painful spot in his life was in his relationship with his adult daughter, whose love and approval he sought constantly but always fell short of obtaining. It always seemed to be just outside Samuel's reach. Maybe, maybe if he did this, or gave her that, then she would forgive him and love him again; that had become Samuel's prayer and mantra. You may be wondering how Samuel's story ends. Samuel enjoyed a life that few of us have the rare privilege to experience—he lived on the water, in a sunny state that kept him warm and happy. He had a close nit group of friends that included me and my husband. Life was marvelous, that is, except for that dark spot, that stain on his life, that *one thing* he could never fix—his relationship with his daughter.

Just as suddenly as his daughter had invited him back into her life when she was twenty, decades later she called Samuel out of the blue with yet another opportunity for him to redeem himself. He could leave the warm, sunny state where he had retired, leave his friends, and move in with his adult-daughter and her family. It wasn't exactly a move-in special. Samuel would help his daughter (now middle aged) buy a large farm. He would help her fulfill a lifetime dream, surely that was worth something. And just so they wouldn't be on top of each other, Samuel would build a guest house on the property; a place for him to live. And to seal the deal, Samuel would put everything in his daughter's name. When it was all said and done, and after all the years of separation and pain, the only thing separating Samuel from his daughter and the family he so yearned to belong to would be a short breezeway between their homes. Redemption was important to Samuel, after all, like all of us, he loved his daughter and wanted/needed to be loved back by her, so the deal was done.

Samuel sold his house on the beach and moved north. He was now in his early seventies and suffered with poor eyesight which prevented him from driving at night. He would essentially become dependent upon his adult daughter. Samuel's friends told him not to do it; more precisely, they emphatically implored him not to do it. And even though Samuel's son was elated at the idea of his father moving closer to him, he too, begged his father not to move in with his estranged sister, warning him that no good could come from it. Samuel's son, along with all his friends thought the move was a bad idea that would only result in more pain for Samuel; after all, there had never been reconciliation or healing, only a constant stream of guilt and payback extracted from Samuel's heart, mind, and wallet over the years. But, in spite of all the advice given to him, Samuel sold everything he owned, bought the property up north, and moved away from his sunny state and all his friends.

What I can tell you about the Samuel that exists today (six years later) is that he is a shell of the bright, creative, funny, happy man we used to know. Although he lives in a brand new guest house that he paid to build with his limited retirement funds, he now sits alone, isolated, lonely, and frequently depressed. The short breezeway that separated his life from his daughter and her family turned out to be a world away from what he hoped for in his twilight years. Last June, Samuel sat alone, expecting some company on Father's Day, but it was not to come. Like Thanksgiving and all the holidays that followed, Samuel was never invited to be a part of the family that lived and celebrated across that breezeway. Samuel's occasional visits to his son are his salvation and do provide love and solace; however, the cruelty of Samuel's situation breaks his son's heart as well as the hearts of those who love him.

Samuel could not fix what was broken in his daughter's mind and heart, and while spending his lifetime attempting to fix, please, and rescue his lost daughter, he lost himself along the way. Samuel story is a living testament to what hatred, animosity, and un-forgiveness can breed. Samuel's family, or what's left of it, has been torn to pieces and remains fragmented, mistrusting, and immersed in pain and conflict to this day.

The lesson for us enablers, fixers, and super-pleasers is that we cannot fix another person's heart or change what they have determined to be true in their minds. We can only mind our own store. When you signed up to be a parent, whether you enlisted or were drafted, you were entrusted with a sacred job, but once you've completed that job, recognize when it's done. You do not *owe* your child/children anything but to authentically love them in a *healthy* manner. And what does authentic or healthy love look like? What does that mean? I can tell you what it does *not* mean. It does not mean that you must endure neglect or abuse from your adult child. You were not called to sacrifice your self esteem, your peace of mind, your money, your friends, your joy, your tranquility, your health, or your sanity for your adult child, particularly if they do not recognize their own love and respect their family, or see in themselves the need to grow and heal and/or if they are being abusive and demanding.

If your child is an adult and you are suffering, chances are that whatever dynamic is wounding you, it did not suddenly appear on the scene from out of nowhere. You more than likely didn't set boundaries a long time ago and you've allowed some pretty awful behavior to go unchecked for some time now. The good news is—it's never too late to show yourself and your child authentic love and respect by setting boundaries around the relationship, or, if the relationship is estranged or nonexistent, to grow new skills and create new ways in which to get the love you crave. As the brilliant Thomas Jefferson, founder and guardian of our country and its freedom once said

"The care of every man's soul belongs to himself."

Remember

Authentic love does not enslave you—it enriches you.
There are no victims—only volunteers.

CHAPTER 8

The Money Game!

It's Your Job to:
Give Me Money—Loan Me Money—Bail Me Out—Pay My Bills—Tolerate My Behavior—And the List Goes on

Being a parent, can at times be like walking a high wire-balance is critical, not only to your emotional and financial survival but to your children's emotional and financial growth and maturity as well. What are you teaching them about respecting you and respecting and developing a responsible relationship with money. When it comes to being a human ATM machine (as one father described himself) There's an old saying that is very true—*'The power others have over me, I give to them.'* Furthermore, the respect you get from others is in direct proportion to the respect you deeply believe you deserve and give to yourself first and then to what you bestow upon others. We all know that if left untended, a garden will fill with weeds, and if kids are left unattended and not properly educated and taught to be responsible, they will live their lives under the false pretense that money grows on some mystical tree you keep hidden in the backyard or in your closet, and that all they need do is *ask*, or in the case of some kids, *demand* it of you. All too often, when parents are in desperate need of attention and approval from their rebelling teen or adult child, they mistakenly think that they can buy love and respect, which reminds us of the famous Beatles lyrics about money—*"Can't buy me love!"* Simple but true.

It's been my experience in interviewing parents that it is those that are obediently seated in either the passenger or back-seat who readily hand over money on demand. As for the parents stuffed in the trunk, money or service is tantamount to ransom that may get you out of the trunk. Parents who are booted from car altogether are likely being punished for saying *"no,"* standing their ground or for defying their child's unreasonable dictates or demands.

We have all played the money game to one degree or another. As a result of my desperate need to be loved and approved of, I had no boundaries in place surrounding money and possessed virtually no ability to say no. In fact, I usually didn't need to be asked, I was more than happy to volunteer both my services and my money. I have seen the same dynamic at play with other parents and recall one overwhelmed mother telling me that on the rare occasions when she did muster up the resolve and courage to just say *no;* the emotional manipulation and outright warfare that took place literally wore her down until finally she caved and gave in. How many of you moms know what I'm talking about? By the way, I am speaking about tweens, teens, and adult children when I speak about abusive behavior, not little ones.

Cheryl, a mother I interviewed, sheepishly shared with me that her otherwise loving and compliant daughter, whenever with her peers or on vacation with her father, would call and be very sweet and attentive to her mother on the phone in order to set the stage for her request for money. If and when that didn't work, she would then become sad and pout. If and when that didn't work, she would then become aggressive in her tone and language. These calls would invariably end in either a concession on mom's part or open hostility and fury, followed by slamming the phone down on the daughter's part. When Cheryl didn't want to or simply was unable to give her daughter what she wanted, her daughter would threaten to take her attention and love away; this would inevitably leave Cheryl shaking and in tears. Sadly, unlike Simon, this mom admitted to almost always giving in. This of course, reinforced the behavior for her daughter and created an environment, or better, a ritual wherein this drama would play itself out over and over again, and always with the same unhealthy behaviors and predictable result. I recall my own adult child, in their early twenties at the time, telling me (not asking me) but telling me that I must perform a service for them. The point was argued vehemently. I thought the request was unreasonable and beyond that, I was especially not okay with the tone and attitude being employed to motivate me, but most shocking of all was the closing argument employed by my teenager who announced—*"It's your job. You owe it to me!"* I was flabbergasted, not so much that my teenager had resorted to that, but that it was clear that my E-generation teenager really believed it to be true. I would later learn that I was not alone. As I polled parents across the country, I found this to be a sentiment/demand echoed over and over by the E-Generation young adults—we *owe* it to them.

One parent tells the story of a son who both wanted and expected a new car for his high school graduation, and indeed he got it. On his very first solo outing in the car, he was involved in a single car accident. Luckily the young man involved was not injured but the new car his parents had bought for him was totaled. This mother and father admit that they pampered and spoiled their son rotten throughout life, and that consequently, he had become a demanding, self-centered tyrant. Within days of the accident, he had another car, and by week's end, he had been involved in another accident. Thankfully, as with the first, no one was hurt in his second accident (except the car). This teen was not exactly what you'd call a conscientious driver; yet amazingly, there were no consequences to his irresponsible behavior. Rather than determine that this young man was not fit to drive yet and call for a much needed time-out in order to establish rules, standards, and expectations for him in order to teach him that vehicle ownership and driving are a privilege to be earned, not a right to be demanded, this teenager was back on the streets in no time. Incredibly, this teenager's car was fully repaired and given back to him with full driving privileges. This marked the third-go-round in the driver's seat within one week, and all with no negative repercussions or consequences.

You can only imagine what the future ultimately holds for these parents. They did share with me that their son not only expected, but would verbally demand money and services from his parents, and when it was not readily given, a tidal wave of name calling, screaming, and verbal abuse routinely followed. In his twenties and still behaving recklessly behind the wheel, their son had received several speeding tickets and consequent increases in insurance premiums. Upset at the escalating cost of insurance for their son's car (i.e., the price *they* were paying in order for their son to continue driving) it was suggested to him that he begin paying his own car insurance premiums as a means of making him a more responsible and safer driver. According to his father, it would be an understatement to say that when it was suggested that he pay his own car insurance premiums, this E-generation son rebelled and exploded with anger at his parents. Name calling, threatening the withdrawal of love and attention, and every other parental gratuity imaginable was held in ransom. Luckily for these parents, they got themselves into counseling and stood their ground. The manipulations, battles, resentment, and abuse on their son's part escalated and lasted for years; there was even a period of total estrangement, and all because these conscientious parents gave up both the keys and driver's seat years earlier (literally in their case) and then later tried to draw a line in the sand.

If that sad but true story doesn't get your attention and drive home the fact that mom and dad must be **parents** (not friends) and that they *must* establish and maintain a healthy family structure and hierarchy, as well as boundaries, perhaps the next story will.

In a case that takes parental authority verses E-generation adult-child entitlement to the extreme edge of demanding behavior and control over one's parent, a New England woman won a lawsuit against her father after he refused to pay for her senior year of college. Yes, you read that correctly, the legal system is amuck with instances where children actually take their parents to task and sue them for a higher education. Why? You know the answer; we established it earlier— because we *owe* it to them, that's why.

Warning: baby boomers who came from Blue Collar backgrounds, with parents who may or may not have graduated from high school and/or were raised with the reality that *they* had to earn their own way in life and that nothing was being given to them on a silver platter (as they so often loved to say) may need to sit down or have someone hold their hand while reading this story.

Following a divorce in 2004, the father of a Southern Connecticut State University student readily agreed to pay for his daughter's college education until she was twenty-five years old. Mom didn't pay a cent towards her daughter's tuition because it was deemed *dad's responsibility,* as it so often is in divorce. (Sorry dads!) Our dad in this story loved his daughter and happily agreed to pay, however, his ex-wife and daughter wanted the agreement *in writing.* Dad complied, but with the caveat that his daughter would apply for student loans and provide him with reliable receipts for her college expenses; sounds fair enough. After paying all of his daughter's tuition and expenses for three years without ever receiving so much as one receipt, and as a result of his daughter never applying for a single student loan, as agreed, the bewildered father in this story, recognizing that his daughter had violated his trust and their agreement, announced that he would *not* pay for a fourth year of college. His daughter, infuriated and indignant about her father's refusal to pay up, sued him. Shockingly (at least to many court-watchers and besieged parents) the judge sided with the daughter, awarding her approximately $50,000. It was time for dear old dad to pay up, and pay up he did, under court-order. A law review journal that offers opinions of socially relevant legal cases declared in utter disbelief and dismay: *"Is this where parent-child relationships are heading?"* Although this case could be considered a 'contract law' case, there are dozens of cases of children suing their parents because they feel entitled to, and owed a higher education, whether or not the parent themselves have been exposed to higher education themselves or can reasonably afford it. This power shift speaks volumes about the new standard of behavior and support expected by an adult child of their parents. My personal view is: whether it's a car or a college education, giving a gift of any kind to a biological relative should be a voluntary byproduct of love and not a court-ordered or E-generation mandate.

Like every other *good parent* out there, I've given money to my children from the abundance of my heart and love and I've also *"loaned"* money to them. Money that, many times, was not paid back, as distinguished from money I've freely given. I've paid off bills that were irresponsibly accrued by my adult child in order to get them out of debt. Like many other caring parents, I have paid for weddings, necessary travel, pleasure trips, vacations, gifts, necessities, or little luxuries my adult children wanted or needed and I've done it happily. I've even had the painful experience of bailing an adult child out of jail, something I pray no parent ever experiences. And now, looking back at it in retrospect, I wish I had done things differently, because although I know I was motivated by my love and generosity, coupled with a desire for the best for my children, I was equally, or perhaps even more motivated by my need to be loved, needed, approved of, and appreciated by my children. Knowing the difference, and coming from an unselfish, healthy place rather than from your neediness is the key to healthy loving and giving. And sometimes, *not giving, not rescuing* or *spoiling*, but rather, *loaning* or requiring your child to achieve or obtain the object of their desire <u>on their own</u> is truly the ultimate expression of healthy parenting and unselfish love for one's child.

The dark side of being a Super-Giver

A funny thing happens when you make yourself *at the ready* to rescue or spoil; your child not only comes to expect and rely upon it, many times, they grow so accustomed to it that they do not appreciate it or respect you for being there for them. In fact, many parents report that ironically, the reverse actually occurs. Strange as it sounds, when you are the *"yes parent"* you are perceived as being *easy to manipulate,* as *weak,* and as someone who can be easily *used* and *manipulated.*

A phenomena that has perplexed mothers the nation over is expressed in the question: why it is that some E-generation children, regardless of their age, tend to walk all over the parent who is always there for them and constantly gives to them, while at the same time, seeking the approval of the parent who is more distant, non-approving, less needy, is not a super-pleaser and cannot be manipulated?

The question is of course, rhetorical. The fact is, it's hard, if not impossible to respect or seek connection with a doormat. The parent with a strong sense of themselves, their value and independence is the parent most likely to earn their child's respect, while the more malleable parent often lacks boundaries and is therefore called upon to meet a child's needs and rescue them, and yet, again, ironically, seldom receives the respect they feel they deserve. This predictable dynamic troubled and perplexed me for many years. It was out of my pain and my pursuit of personal and spiritual growth that the answer finally came to me.

> *Deep down in the consciously unaware recesses of their minds and hearts, children actually want and need a parent who is endowed with a deep sense of self-worth and self-respect; a parent who is strong for themselves and their children, and who, via those qualities has established stalwart boundaries relative to how they allow themselves to be treated and what behavior is and is not acceptable from their children.*

A Doormat's Dilemma

Let's admit it, we moms are usually the family doormat, but, to our credit, wondrously, we mothers love our families one-hundred percent, and we do that with all our heart, mind, body, and soul. We are conditioned since conception to give everything of ourselves. No matter how good a father is, he can never know what sacrifices a mother makes for her child, from conception to birth, and from birth to the grave. Mothers are a special breed, a unique species unto ourselves. But, in an ironic and often painful twist, the very qualities that make us incredibly loving, generous, and committed to our children (often to extreme levels of self denial and blind devotion) are the very qualities that bring unbelievable suffering into our lives.

To bail out or not to bail out—That is the question

Many broken hearted parents, including myself, have gotten *'the call!'* You know the one I'm talking about; it usually comes in the middle of the night or when you have company over. You only faintly recognize the voice on the other end of the phone as being that of your older teenage or adult-child, that's because it's the voice of a small, frightened child who you haven't heard from in years; it is the voice of a child who suddenly loves, respects, and needs you desperately. And what happens next? If you're like me or most mothers out there, you drop everything and race off to mortgage your home and rescue your wayward child. A staggering number of these *'please bail me out'* calls are made directly to moms across the country. Women as opposed to men get this call because most children instinctively know they have a direct line to mom's heart. It is a statistical fact that when older teens or young adult males get themselves in trouble and find themselves behind bars there's one person they almost always call first, and *who* is that? *Their mommas, that's who!*

Some parents have resolved long ago that should their child ever be arrested, and should such a call ever come, they will not bail their child out, and their teen or adult child knows this. I do not presume to have the definitive answer but will share that of the parents polled, there is a clear split as to what's best for the child. Some say, let them spend a night in jail, and others will sell their souls to make bond for their child. A couple of things I've learned as a result of my own experience is that if the adult child is not held responsible for their actions either by the community or their family, and if they are not required to repay the non-refundable portion of their bail, no lesson is learned and the attitude that gave birth to the behavior is seldom corrected because you cannot correct or heal what you refuse to acknowledge and address. Being strong, lovingly setting boundaries, and maintaining them in a spirit of love can be hard to do as we'll see in the next story.

Kathryn's Story

Kathryn, by all accounts, had been a loving and conscientious single-parent who had a secure job she loved, complete with a 401K, retirement, and wonderful work associates. She also had a healthy, supportive network of friends in her life and community and was preparing to buy her first home. She was elated and excited with the direction her life was taking.

Kathryn had always provided a good home for her only-child, a daughter. She had given her everything she could; however, Kathryn did not set proper boundaries and unfortunately tolerated escalating levels of challenging/disrespectful behavior on the part of her teenage daughter. It started with verbal assaults and emotional estrangement and was followed by at-risk behavior, multiple piercing and tattoos. This was only the beginning for this mother and daughter. When Kathryn found out (via a call from the school) that her daughter had dropped out of high school, Kathryn was stunned and determined to rectify the situation immediately, but to her shock, she discovered that she was powerless to stop her daughter from dropping out of high school. As she discovered, the prevailing laws in the state where they lived allowed minors sixteen years of age and older to drop out of high school without a parent's approval. In an odd juxtaposition of priorities, a minor, if caught smoking in public, was in a considerable amount of trouble with the law, yet they could dis-enroll from school at will with absolutely no legal or societal repercussions. Kathryn was beside herself. When she attempted to impose her will and demand that the unruly teen return to school, her mandate was met with open defiance. Being a super-pleaser and wanting to avoid confrontation, mom backed down. Talk about a major power shift in the household. What to do? Kathryn could not throw her own child out on the streets; she loved her too much to do that and would never even threaten such a consequence. At a total loss of what to do, Kathryn relented, recoiled, and then retired into a corner where she no longer had any input or power inside the relationship. She surrendered the keys, the car, and even the driver's seat in one sweeping defeat and surrender of arms.

Time passed and Kathryn's daughter became engaged to her first-love, a childhood friend from the neighborhood. Years earlier, the boy's family had moved to the other side of the country but he and his former high school sweetheart remained in contact. Settled into a new job she loved and ready to close on her first home, Kathryn was again shaken to her core when her daughter announced that she was going to move across country to be with her fiancé.' The only problem was: her daughter did not own a car, had no money to pay for the trip, and no one on the other side of the country was willing or able to come get her or finance her relocation. When Kathryn's daughter began imploring her to take her across country, Kathryn said no. Although she could not keep her daughter from withdrawing from high school, she was determined not to condone a teenage marriage. Additionally, being new to her job, Kathryn had not accrued vacation time and could not, and would not give up her job or the new home she was buying in order to fulfill her daughter's wishes. Upon hearing that her mother would not drive her across country, Kathryn's daughter quickly began emotionally leveraging her mother by telling her mother that she knew she'd say no because she had always known that her mother didn't love her enough, that she *(the daughter)* didn't matter enough because mom's job and new house were more important than she was. The game not only was *on*, it would be played both artfully and full-out.

After allowing those seeds of guilt to settle into her mind and heart, the fear bomb was dropped when Kathryn's daughter announced that it was okay that her mother didn't want to take her—she would simply hitchhike across country alone. Well, the mere idea of her beautiful teenage daughter hitchhiking across country was more than enough to move mom in the direction her daughter wanted. Kathryn, out of her abundance of love and a desire to please her daughter and earn the love she so craved in return, as well as out of profound sense of worry and dread over what could befall her daughter if she left on her own, quit her job, pulled out of the purchase of her first home, sold everything she owned, and drove her daughter across country to be with her fiancé.' For those of you who may be asking why Kathryn didn't just buy a plane ticket and send her daughter on her way, it was because Kathryn's daughter was under age; she was still a minor and would require a guardian while she awaited her eighteenth birthday, when she could then legally marry without her mother's approval. It's quite a paradox to say that a mother would not approve of a teen-marriage but could be leveraged to take her daughter across country to await her eighteenth birthday but that is exactly what Kathryn did.

When contemplating this complex situation, it's worth noting that Kathryn was one of the walking wounded. She admits to being a mother who took the *'friend'* route with her daughter rather than embodying the role of parent and its duties. She did not set boundaries around what was and was not acceptable behavior. More than anything else, Kathryn craved her daughter's love and approval, and it would be those deep-seated needs that would over-ride her common sense and parental instincts.

Once committed to the trip, Kathryn thought it would be cathartic and result in a healing and major shift in her relationship with her daughter. Kathryn felt hopeful; after all, who wouldn't love and appreciate someone who gave up *everything* for them (their job, their home, their belongings, money, time, friends, etc.). Kathryn felt sure that having made such a huge, life-altering sacrifice for her daughter, that she would finally win the love and approval she so desperately craved from her, but, like Samuel, she did not. In fact, in her interview, Kathryn reported that as the years passed, her daughter's controlling behavior grew worse until finally the relationship completely disintegrated. Kathryn had naively hoped that by sacrificing of herself and by giving all her love and respect to the one she craved it from the most, that it would be automatically reciprocated; it was not. Ironically, it had the opposite affect and set in motion years of emotional abuse and neglect. Who's to blame here? I believe it is *mom*. After all, admittedly, Kathryn gave up her role as parent a long-long time ago when she gave up the driver's seat and was content to take her place in the passenger seat; a place she comfortably occupied for a short while. As time went on, Kathryn was content to sit in the back and grab for a crumb of love or respect from her daughter, and as she did that, she became more and more needy and less and less a person worthy of an adult child's respect.

Kathryn, like many of us moms, had effectively taught her daughter how to treat her; she did that by not respecting herself first and foremost. And then, later in life, when she stood her ground around powerful issues, Kathryn was promptly placed in the trunk and pulled out on an as-needed basis only. I hold Kathryn responsible because she did not established healthy, respectful boundaries and lovingly enforce them early on. Kathryn willingly gave up the driver's seat and like many before her, was ultimately tossed out along the highway and is now among the walking wounded of America's discarded and disowned parents.

My Story

I spent fifteen long and grueling years in a physically and emotionally abusive marriage. During those fifteen years, I was physically beaten and worn down emotionally and spiritually. I lived in a state of fear and trepidation on a daily basis. My husband expected and demanded absolute respect and submission from both me and later, our small children, and he got it! A spirit of anxiety and fear permeated our home. Emotional and physical abuse began within weeks of our civil service and continued for the duration of the marriage. Later in life, when asked why I didn't just up and leave, I would share the painful story of having been unwillingly married—off to a foster brother by my unsophisticated, howbeit well-meaning mother when I was just sixteen years old. At that young age, and with no life experiences, confidence, resources, or extended family to go to, I had no options. After four years in an arranged, loveless marriage, my desire and acute need to experience genuine love and connection was met by the birth of my first child. Two and a-half years later, I was blessed with my second child. My children were my *all* and *everything* and I loved them beyond all else and was selflessly devoted to them. They were my singular source of love, validation, worthiness, identity; they were my very reason for living.

Unknown to me, in the midst of our dysfunctional and abusive home environment, a critical infra-structure and familial hierarchy had been firmly established and reinforced without my knowing it. My children grew up watching their mother be beaten, verbally demeaned, and emotionally manipulated and tormented. I had become a silent, voiceless victim in our home. Fear and an anxious quietness had become the norm in our family and in our house. I clung more desperately than ever to the only solid, reliable thing I had—my children. I had always wanted to go, to flee. I had wanted my children and I to be free for years but was intimidated and afraid. I would learn later in counseling that I suffered from *battered wife's syndrome*. I had been entirely dependent on this man for fifteen years and was afraid to leave because I had no resources, no job skills, no one to turn to and nowhere to go, or so I thought. In addition to that, for years my husband had threatened to end his life if I ever left him (the ultimate form of emotional blackmail). That was a lot to overcome, but, once the abuse directly touched the lives of my children, I left and never looked back.

I know now that the abuse affected my children the very first time they witnessed it. They were experiencing it too, even if the bulk of it was directed toward me. It affected them just as much as it would have, had they been the recipients of the abuse themselves. It affected them profoundly to see a powerless, frightened mother attempting to pretend everything was alright and always trying to shield them from their father's moods and violent outbreaks. But, having married at sixteen, and never having any real life experiences or support, I was so isolated that, at the time, I was grateful that my husband's physical abuse was aimed primarily at me during the years that preceded my departure.

At the time I left, my entire life experience up to that point had been very one dimensional. I had been with this abusive/damaged person since I was sixteen years old and was completely financially dependent on him. I had no education and had never worked outside the home, and to make the situation more challenging, I had no family available to help me out. Suddenly, it was me and my two young children alone in the world.

I tell this story purely for the purpose of sharing with you the emotional history and dynamics that set me up to be emotionally abused and neglected for years to come, and this time, it would be my children who played out the role their father crafted and modeled so consistently for them for so many years. I remained a victim by not breaking the pattern that had been set in place so many years earlier. Please hear that again and take note—**I did not break the pattern!** Their entire lives, my children witnessed their mother being treated in a very specific, very demeaning and disrespectful way, and when we finally left and set up a household of our own, although the threat of physical abuse no longer existed for my children, peace and harmony only lasted a short while. Before long, a shift occurred when that unconditional mommy love we spoke of earlier got married to my neediness and desire to be *everything* to my kids and to make up for their painful past. I vigorously endeavored to become my children*'s best friend* so as to ensure that I would be liked, loved, approved of, and accepted in their lives. Although I loved them with all my heart, I was not the strong parent they needed desperately and they had never learned to respect me. To make matters worse, I rationalized that by allowing my children to vent their oppressed feelings of anger and resentment on me, I was me being a *good parent* via exercising what I thought was *unconditional love.* I was allowing them to be 'self-expressed toward me, something they could never do with their father, and by self-expressed, I don't just refer to the healthy form of self expression but to allowing such things as name calling, abusive or condescending tones of voice, demeaning remarks, and emotional blackmail. Rather than establishing a new and empowered identity for myself as someone who deserved and required respect, I allowed destructive behavior to develop and persist. I failed to recognize that because of our particular history of family dysfunction, coupled with E-generation challenges, I needed to establish new rules and boundaries, as well as a new and strong self-identity for our new life together. Unknowingly, what I allowed (in the name of love and self expression) became a recipe for disaster.

I spent years being at my children's beck and call, forgiving and *understanding* the verbal abuse, and all the while being overly, even excessively generous, and often without appreciation or even recognition of my love, support, and generosity. My life became a vicious cycle of me seeking love, acceptance, approval, and respect from my children as if my life depended on it. Ironically, yet logically, the more and the harder I tried, the more elusive it became. I became a full-fledged, consummate *victim,* or more accurately, I remained the victim they had grown up with. I did not grow but instead, I shrank away little by little.

Finally, for me, I realized that for all those times that I didn't set boundaries, didn't say *no* when I should have (and stick with it), when I allowed disrespectful behavior and language to go unchecked because I believed that *unconditional love* and acceptance would pay off in the end, **I was dead wrong.** Furthermore, what I was doing was NOT a loving act toward my children; it was quite the opposite. I also learned that there are no victims in life, only volunteers. I was definitely a volunteer and a completely codependent enabler. I was not only cultivating but encouraging, even rewarding the neglectful, abusive behaviors I abhorred so much. The very behavior I fled from when I left my husband, the very behavior I thought I was saving my children from, would, howbeit less violently, play itself out again and again in our lives, but this time, the painful behaviors and abuse would occur within the relationships I cherished the most and with the people I loved the most—my children. And saddest of all, it would happen within the clearly constructed framework established and modeled for my children by their father years earlier, a framework and pattern I did not identify and de-construct.

By the way, one of life's crazy footnotes: like a cold hard slap in the face, I spent years bemoaning the fact that I was the *'good parent.'* I was always there; I unconditionally loved my children; I gave them everything that was within my power to give; I routinely forgave less-than-admirable behavior; I never abused my children; I did this, I did that, and the list went on, and on, and on, and yet, at the end of the day, who do you think was the recipient of an almost religious quest on the part of my children to win their love and respect? The very love and respect I so craved. You got it—their father.

Although my children's father was abusive, and although he was neglectful when it came to positive re-enforcement for his children, he did one thing exceptionally well and he did it consistently, he demanded absolute and total respect. In our household, respect was not negotiable, nor would he tolerate any lack thereof. That was an *absolute* and my children knew it and respected it, period. His line in the sand was immovable. Aside from my continued commitment to my victim role and lack of personal growth, it would also be true to say that we moms usually have not drawn an immovable line in the sand, in fact, we move the line all the time, don't we? And we wonder why we seem to be at the short end of the respect stick at the end of the day. So what, if anything can we take or learn from these stories? Here's the deal mom, it boils down to three big things:

1—You must determine what your definition of love is and whether it's a healthy one. What I've learned is that love does not equal indulgence or the allowance of unacceptable behavior (for any reason!). Genuine, authentic love for both yourself and your children means that you love and respect yourself and your role as woman and mother first and foremost. After all, if you don't love and respect yourself, no one else is going to do it for you, especially your children. In fact, they'll resent the weakness in you. You must also establish a family structure (especially if you're a single mother) wherein you are the authority figure, period. A place where you are your child's PARENT and not their wanna-be friend. Remember these three important facts about you, your kid, and friendships: 1) they have lots of friends already. 2) Throughout their lifetime friends will come and go. 3) They only have one mother and you're it, and you're there for life.

2—It's your job to create an environment where it's not only okay, but essential that you say *"NO"* when you need to, and mean it. Your children must know that the buck stops with you. And that money tree-yank it out by its roots; you're not doing your child any favors by encouraging a sense of laziness or cultivating a narcissist who feels it's not only your job but your duty fulfill their expectations. Your duty is to teach them the art of self-reliance, fiscal responsibility, and a work ethic that includes earning things instead of having them handed to them on a platter. You must teach your child that it is both a good thing and an absolute essential that they learn to accomplish and acquire some things on their own in this life. They must learn that they are responsible for their actions, errors, and screw ups. It is one of the most important ways that you can truly love and nurture your child regardless of their age.

3—If, like me, and many other well-meaning but *needy* moms, you have loved and desperately needed a *love payback* in return;

you may have given up the driver's seat or are vying for a place in the *best friend* category rather than being a parent and doing what is ultimately best for our child's emotional/social growth. You may have already created an unhealthy relationship or power shift relative to your teen or adult child, if so, all that means is that RIGHT NOW is the time to break any unhealthy patterns that exist.

Breaking the pattern simply means taking one or two of the unhealthy relationship dynamics and drawing the proverbial line in the sand. Start small if you have to, but please, set up some boundaries for yourself and your child. Take baby steps and applaud your own efforts and progress. And remember, you are not leaving your child, nor are you denying them love or betraying them, in fact, you are doing the opposite, you are demonstrating love, love for them, and perhaps for the first time in years, love and respect for yourself.

Know in advance and accept that it will be hard and may even be grossly unpleasant when you give up your fixer, super-giver, doormat, or victim identity, but, remember, you are the one who set things up the way they were (and are presently) and beyond that, you have more than likely re-enforced and even rewarded the behaviors you find unacceptable and/or hurtful now. Acknowledge and accept responsibility for that and become determined to break any negative patterns, replacing them with a new, healthy environment for yourself and ultimately for your child too (even though they may not appreciate it now). If your child is an adult, that means it is time to focus on *you* and your growth. Remember the self respect we talked about earlier? Take a look at yourself and examine your own level of self respect, self appreciation, and determine where you're at right now. And most importantly, remember that the love and respect you crave must come from you first, and from there, it will spread to others.

CHAPTER 9

The Demand—Do It MY WAY or Else!

When it's
'My Way or The Highway'—Take the Highway!

If nothing else, I hope we've learned that when tantrums are thrown and ultimatums issued, whether they are dictated by tweenies, teenagers, or adult children, instead of folding like a deck of cards (as we usually do) we parents need to stand our ground. We must do this because it is the right thing to do and because it truly is *love in action*, and if that doesn't convince you, just take a look at your own history or the stories shared in this book; if nothing else, they have painfully demonstrated and hopefully taught us that allowing ourselves to become a human target, doormat, ATM, or indentured servant who believes that one day your debt will be paid off or the love and respect you crave so deeply will finally be yours, does not work, is not the truth, and is not what you deserve. It is not what your child needs or deserves either, so quit feeding the monster and then complaining when it tears the house down.

As parents of one or more E-generation children, you more than likely have experience in this department and could probably share a tale or two of your own. Don't get me wrong, creating, sharing, and sustaining any love, whether it's the love shared between partners, parent and child, siblings, or friends requires commitment, work, and maintenance, but with two distinctions from the unhealthy emotional enslavement some of our parents have been describing. The two most notable observations and distinctions are:

1) The love and respect exchanged between the parties is mutual and reciprocated. Healthy love is meant to be flexible, respectful, and freely flows in multiple directions. When it is forced down a one-way street, it won't be long before the one doing all the relationship care-taking, loving, giving and forgiving becomes emotionally and physically exhausted, and eventually burns out.

2) In a healthy love state, violations of human/family core values and mutual needs are inconceivable to the parties and are therefore not practiced because love, as well as nurturing and preservation of the relationship is paramount.

When those dynamics do not voluntarily exist side by side as pillars in a relationship it becomes counter-intuitive and counter-productive to simply continue to coexist in that kind neglectful or even harmful environment. It makes as much sense as giving into a bully who insists on having things their way at all times and calling those concessions part of a healthy relationship. Existing in that kind of emotional wasteland is not healthy and it is not authentic, healthy love. If you are indeed a parent who has suffered with either verbal abuse or has been thrown into the back seat or trunk, I want you to consider your acquaintances and friendships for a moment. Were a friend or acquaintance to treat you the way your teen or adult-child does, would they continue to be your friend? Yes or no? And beyond that, since there is a 50%-plus divorce rate in America (higher among blended families), I'd wager a bet that if your spouse or partner consistently conducted themselves in an abusive or woefully neglectful manner, and after satisfying yourself that you'd tried everything possible to salvage the relationship, you would relieve yourself of that relationship—yes or no?

My own life experiences and those of my friends and colleagues suggest that you would not stay in an unhealthy, neglectful, or abusive relationship but that you might try (depending on the specific relationship and your disposition toward it) to salvage the relationship but if not successful, eventually you would move on, sometimes happily, sometimes regretfully but move on, you would. You most certainly would not tolerate bad behavior from a stranger or acquaintance and although you may tolerate it for a while from a friend or intimate, absent some severe self esteem issues, you more than likely would not tolerate it for long. As we shared earlier, statistics show that even when a couple takes a vow before God to love, honor, and put up with each other's shenanigans for the rest of their lives or until death does them part, they too, will eventually draw a line in the sand if a core value is being violated, and will, if deemed necessary, leave the very relationship they promised to stay in forever.

So why is it, we parents will tolerate some of the worst treatment we will ever receive in our lives, and from our own children no less, and yet, we keep coming back for more? We won't take it from stranger, acquaintances, friends, or even our partner, but we will from our children? Why is that so? Our children are the only human beings on earth from whom we will tolerate all manner of abuse and not only will we keep coming back for more, we often encourage and reward the behavior, and that's because we mistakenly believe that somewhere in the sacred parental code of ethics it states that *no matter what,* we must continue to behave in a loving and accepting way towards our children as if they were still toddlers who are not responsible for their actions and should not be held accountable. There is a prevailing logic and it's an unreasonable logic of the heart echoed by wounded, battle fatigued mothers everywhere and it goes like this—we are mothers and are, as thus, hardwired to identify *tolerance* (even under horrific circumstances) as *unconditional love* or as *our duty,* but is that what it really is?

I would dare to suggest to you that LOVE does not behave itself that way. Authentic love/Healthy love does not invoke or support this kind of behavior. From my experience, interviews, and research, I am convinced that it is not love but FEAR that holds parents hostage in these kinds of unhealthy and even abusive relationships with their children. Fear of being unloved. Fear that if we step up to the plate or put on our parent boots back on, we will be loathed, rejected and/or totally abandoned. It is a profound fear of the unknown; fear of rejection; fear of not being loved and valued, that's what paralyzes us the most. Why is fear such a powerful influence in our lives and relationships? I believe it is because: for most of us, including you, rejection from your own child, the one human being in whom you've invested all your love, hope, and trust, your very flesh and blood (or the child you chose through adoption), the single person you've nurtured, protected, cared for, and selflessly served their entire life . . . rejection from this person would be so overwhelming and emotionally devastating that it MUST be avoided at all costs, even if the price you pay and the precious commodity you risk is your mental, physical, spiritual or financial health and welfare. The lower your own sense of *'self'* and *self esteem*, the more vulnerable you are, and the more susceptible you are to tolerating/excusing inappropriate or abusive behavior. That is also why, when your child deeply wounds you, and does it repeatedly or rejects you completely, that act of abandonment carries with it a deep and profound meaning for you. Nearly every parent I interviewed for this book has said virtually the same thing—*'if my own child rejects me, I am valueless. I am a bad parent and a bad person.'* That is a very big, ugly, and painful pill to swallow and it chokes the life out of you going down. It's also the reason parents allow unhealthy relationships not only to persist but to flourish with their adult children.

Beyond that, and what is true for many parents, especially those whose very identity is closely tied to, or is singularly defined as being a mother (or father), rejection from their child/children is tantamount to emotional death because, for these parents, if their child rejects them, their very sense of *'self,'* *'self worth,'* and *'purpose'* are at risk of being annihilated. This happens because, at their core, being a mother (or father) is genuinely and entirely who they are as human beings, and to be denied that identity irreparably cripples the mind and wounds the spirits of these parents. These are the parents who are at the greatest risk of suffering empty nest syndrome, clinical depression, substance abuse or self medicating, as well as suicidal ideology and/or attempts in order to lessen the pain and garner the attention they crave from their children. That potential reality is a frightening prospect and a cautionary warning that we would all do well to heed.

When you consider those kinds of emotional consequences and pain, doesn't it seem easier to fall in line and go with the flow, take the hits, settle for any crumbs that may fall your way, smile through the pain, and hope that one day it will get better? Isn't that why we as parents call it 'love' that motivates us to act as we do? When in reality, it is a combination of our intrinsic/instinctual love coupled with a debilitating fear that we will lose ourselves if we lose our connection to our children, no matter how one-sided, negative, or even abusive that connection may be. But the truth is, deep down, we know, I know and you know that healthy love and parental respect does not behave itself that way. We know that in any other situation or with any other human being on earth we would not tolerate the conditions we are living in. So let's get real and see that as much as or perhaps more than love, it is low self esteem coupled with a lack of proper parenting skills and boundary setting, and fear that governs our behavior and keep us in this pattern.

Do not confuse the dysfunctional, unhealthy love we are addressing with the love most families experience, families that experience combinations of ups and downs, highs and lows, happiness and sadness, challenges, victories and defeat, elation and upset. We are addressing relationships that are neglectful, controlling, harmful and abusive; relationships where those involved are suffering. Although we applaud and envy normal/high functioning families that enjoy healthy relations, we are concerned with the latter.

Now, for those of you in the latter group, first, as I've said before and will again, know that you're not alone, and that you're not a bad person or inferior parent. Try, if you can, to begin to see that it is your very sense of self-worth, self esteem, and purpose that's being called into question as a consequence of the issues and pain you are experiencing with your child. Know also that you are now in the unique position of choosing the path of rigorous honesty, both with yourself and your child. You can choose self-exploration, introspection, revelation, and self growth that can result in a major transformation of your life. You can also become a profound force for good in your own life and the lives of those you love, but only if you take this on as an opportunity for personal growth. Start with honesty and move forward, reminding yourself that you cannot change what you refuse to acknowledge. Take heart fellow mothers and friends and know that we're going to work through this process together, and along that lonely stretch of highway, we will discover new things about ourselves. We will learn how to develop other sources of love, connection, and validation in our lives while establishing and maintaining healthy boundaries and authentic love for ourselves and our children. Rather than buying into or sustaining drama or pain, we will make new and healthy choices that will benefit us and ultimately our children and everyone in our lives.

Love is a Verb—not an Adjective
Love is not something we simply say or describe
It's something we <u>Do</u>

CHAPTER 10

Making Children Pawns in Divorce
Parental Sabotaging 101

Let me first say, I hope the parents reading this book have not engaged in this selfish and destructive behavior, and if you are— STOP, NOW!

One of the saddest causalities of divorce is a child's sense of security, innocence, and safe/reliable love. When one or both parents decide to use their child as a weapon to hurt their former partner, everyone gets hurt, but without exception the heart and soul that suffers the most damage is that of the child stuck in the middle. It must be recognized and emphasized that using children as pawns, whatever the reason or circumstance, is reprehensible and does not pay off, not in the now, and not in the future. The fact is, using your child as either leverage or as an instrument of pain or revenge relative to your former partner is one of the single most selfish, destructive crimes a parent can commit against their child.

Ron's story

I have met and consoled many parents whose relationship with their child has been utterly destroyed as the result of sabotaging on the part of the other parent/ex-spouse. One of the divorced parents I spoke with while researching this book shared with me that when his wife announced that she had been seeing someone else and was leaving, their child was only two years old. It was a very bitter and acrimonious divorce that resulted in a long and painful custody battle because the child's mother wanted to whisk the toddler away to another state, thousands of miles away, so she could join her lover there. Broken hearted over his wife's deception and betrayal, Ron was fighting to keep his little girl in the state and in his life. During the course of litigation and after the case was decided in Ron's favor (i.e., his ex-wife could not leave the state), his former spouse grew bitter and resentful because her plans had been disrupted, and all because of Ron's determination to keep his little girl in his life. Ron may have succeeded in keeping his daughter in the state but could never have imagined how his ex would act-out as a result of not winning the case and getting her way. Ron's daughter, just two years old at the time, was subjected to constant verbal brainwashing by her mother. Ironically, in spite of the fact that according to Ron, it was his wife who violated the wedding vows and left the marriage, *he* was viewed as the bad guy and enemy because he interrupted the *happy ending* planned by the new couple. Ron became the target of his former wife's wrath, with the weapon used to exact revenge being their two-year old toddler.

Over time, an open, loving, and demonstrative toddler was turned into a guarded/mistrusting stranger to her father. The two major contributing factors in this tragedy were the time literally lost with his daughter at such an impressionable, tender age coupled with the demeaning and inflammatory remarks that were continually made to his daughter by his Ron's ex-wife. Paradoxically, to make matters worse, Ron was very easy-going and passive. Because of his non-confrontational nature, Ron simply did not know how to compete with or combat the outspoken, aggressive, and vengeful nature of the parent who chose to use their child as a weapon. Sadly, Ron's story is not special or extraordinary. Forcing a child to 'take sides' or out-right attempts to turn the child against one of his or her parents happens far too often in our culture. In Ron's case, he came to realize and appreciate that a full-fledged war had been waged against him, and that what was at risk was his child's love and emotional health, as well as any relationship he hoped to share with his young daughter in the present and certainly into the future. Deciding it was imperative that he take action, Ron got himself and his little girl into counseling where they worked hard to build an honest, healthy, loving and supportive rapport and trust regardless of the continued attempts of his ex-wife to measure, compete with, and sabotage their relationship. In a dramatic and tragic twist, after four years of what both father and daughter described as a joyous, loving, and supportive relationship (one they worked hard to create) the young lady confided that her mother would punish her emotionally if she spoke well of Ron or his new wife and that whenever she reported having a good time or a great visit with her father, the wrath she incurred was more than she could bear. After being continually prodded to choose sides and devote her loyalties to her mother, and suffering the consequences when she didn't, the young lady in this story, Ron's beloved daughter, told him that she could no longer "*be in the middle*"—that she *"can't take it anymore"* and at age 12, boldly told her father that she never wanted to see him again. Hoping that her sacrifice and cruelty to her father would make peace for her at home with her mother, this once bright and loving daughter (whose father fought so tenaciously for her) tossed him under a bus and broke his heart into uncountable pieces in order to demonstrate her love and devotion to her mother. Although this kind of sabotaging can take place at any age, to intentionally corrupt the heart and mind of a toddler is criminal, if not downright evil; it also leads me to one of the most wide spread, heart wrenching and destructive things a custodial parent can do to the ex and to their child, and that is to discredit, emotionally disqualify, or attempt to erase the non-custodial parent altogether.

Giving credit where credit is due—whether you like it or not!

Note: In this next section, for the purpose of literary clarity, I have chosen to refer to the libeled and injured parent as 'father'; however, mother is interchangeable, depending on which parent is guilty of sabotaging.

If you are divorced and if it's been a particularly hurtful and bitter breakup and custody battle—are you speaking ill of your former partner in front of your young, impressionable child? Are you intentionally trying to pollute their hearts and minds and turn them against their father? Do you undermine? Do you attempt to supplant your child's father with your latest partner? Do you receive regular child-support payments but offer not the slightest credit to your ex for helping to support *their child,* as well as the child's interests, and needs? Do you lie to your child about their father? Do you accidentally forget to tell your ex about school plays, projects, performances, doctor's appointments or meetings? Do you take all the credit for the things you tell your child *you* provide for them, even though that is not true? Do you even go so far as to tell your child that their father does not care about them and/or does not contribute to their life, when in fact, you are only able to provide for them either in part or perhaps entirely because of the financial contribution of your child's father? If you've answered *yes* to any of these questions, then let me first scold you by saying *shame on you for depriving your child of experiencing the love and support of their father.* Whether this occurs because we are woman and therefore are inherently possessive and territorial, even about our children, or simply because we're hurt and bitter and want to hurt back, or whether it's a crime perpetrated by the custodial parent regardless of their gender (and women just happen to get custody most the time) remains unclear and doesn't really matter. What is sadly and anecdotally clear is that woman/mothers are the *'at fault'* party most of the time, and that's a shame.

Do the right thing

Regardless of what has happened between you and your ex, you both created the child you now share together, and now owe it to your child (not each other) . . . *to your child,* to allow them to experience the love and support of *both* of their parents. So stop the maligning and begin to give credit where credit is due. If your child takes karate, ballet or horseback riding lessons, whatever it is, let them know that it's <u>not just you</u> that's making that possible; it's you *and dad,* or you and mom (if that's the case) that are doing this for them because you both love them. Don't do to your child or grandchildren what Samuel and Ron's ex-wives did to their daughters' minds and hearts; be kinder, wiser, and more enlightened than that. Love your child enough to give them the greatest gift you have at your disposal to bestow—the gift of allowing them to freely love and acknowledge their fathers. Your child will grow up a happier, more secure human being, and you will have gone a long way towards creating a mutually loving and supportive environment in which that can happen, and that's something you can be proud of regardless of the actions of your former spouse.

This kind of ugly sabotaging can occur at any age. I have seen it happen with toddlers, young children, and teenagers, as well as with adult children. And, it is most certainly not a torture reserved for fathers only. I recall the case of Sharon, whose daughter was fifteen when she and her husband divorced. Again, the same scenario played itself out. One parent chose the high ground and put the child first, whereas the other, out of anger, pain, resentment, or some other emotional disorder, chose to sacrifice their own child sense of security and emotional welfare in exchange for exercising their own need for revenge. Full time efforts where exerted to make this young woman see her mother as a villain who had abandoned the family, when actually, the woman's husband had been cheating for years and she had finally had enough. Because of her level of personal integrity and out of concern for her daughter, Sharon was determined not to lower her standards by saying anything negative about her daughter's father/her former husband. Sharon took what she thought was the moral high ground but lost her daughter. There was so much negative input regularly given to her daughter (things that were outright lies designed to turn the daughter against her mother) that ultimately, the daughter involved in this situation decided to live with her father, and acted out in horrible ways towards her mother whenever she would see her.

Sharon's heart was broken. She simply could not wrap her mind around what was happening. When she was encouraged to tell her daughter the truth, she declined, adamantly saying that she did not want to lower herself or her standards to her ex-husbands' base level of behavior, nor did she (as a mother) want her daughter to think poorly of her father, which is admirable and is what a true mother's love does, but guess what happened? Sharon succeeded! She protected her ex-husband's reputation and allowed her own to be destroyed. The young lady in this story continued to grow further and further from a mother with whom she was once incredibly close and loved dearly; she also continued to hear awful things about her mother from her father. Eventually, this young lady grew more and more troubled, ultimately turning to alcohol and drugs for relief from her family pain and drama.

Personally, I am an advocate of practicing honesty with children, and the older they are, the more objective but rigorous the honesty should be. With rare exceptions, and then, only for the benefit of the child, should a truth be withheld. Secrets are almost always about shame on some level or another and shame has no business in a healthy relationship, either with others or with oneself. That being said, outside of qualifying circumstances, I am all for telling children the complete truth, whatever it may be. Of course, depending on their age and the severity of conditions they're living in or exposed to, your communications must be tailored to suit their needs and be age-appropriate. I have yet to come across an instance or situation where allowing lies and defamation to prevail or allowing yourself to become a living martyr was either healthy or paid off in the end. And when I say *"paid off"*—I am not talking about a pay-off for you, I'm talking about this behavior paying off emotionally for the child involved, and then, secondarily, the fact that it will not pay off for you.

Not all parents are equipped with the skills and emotional objectivity to carry this off. In those instances, I recommend getting hooked up with a qualified/gifted counselor. FYI—All licensed counselors are *'qualified'* but not all therapists are *gifted*. By that, I mean that they are not blessed with the gift of being truly empathetic practitioners who sincerely care for their patients or possess the ability to read behavior, offer meaningful insights, and help guide a patient to a healing place. Ideally you want a counselor who will challenge you to grow as a parent, and most importantly will challenge you to grow personally and to learn to know, love, trust, and honor yourself as the unique, special individual you are. Do not settle for finding someone you simply pay just to listen to you and empathize with your pain—*you have friends who can do that for free.* If you opt for counseling, shop for a counselor just the way you would for a car. Do your homework, conduct research, ask for references, ask important questions, kick the tires, take them for a test drive, and if the fit is not right or your gut says *no,* don't settle—keep looking!

CHAPTER 11

Love Held Hostage

When Grandchildren Are Used As Pawns

"A grandchild is God's reward for raising a child."—Bill Cobsy

If you have lost contact with your grandchild as a result of family drama and estrangement, let me first wrap my love around you, give you a deep and enduring spiritual embrace, and tell you that your broken heart is cradled in the hands of God and in the hearts of all who read this book.

When grandchildren, the most innocent of all family members are held as emotional ransom or used as pawns to wage war, control, leverage, or *'get even'* with an offending (or perceived as offending grandparent) no one wins and everyone loses, especially the grandchildren. Why our adult children, who are parents themselves, are willing to put their own selfish need to inflict pain on their parents/grandparents is beyond my comprehension and I would hazard to guess, is well beyond the comprehension of most balanced, mature, conscientious, and caring human beings. Providing you were/are a well-meaning, responsible grandparent who has done nothing but love and be there for both your children and your grand-babies, the pain imposed on your heart and soul when you are ostracized from your grandchildren's lives is akin to the grief one suffers after a death. It can be overwhelming and debilitating. If a grandparent is suddenly and/or maliciously booted out of their grandchildren's life, especially if there was no cause or catalyst for the ejection that they are aware of for the dissolution of the relationship, a thoughtful, loving grandparent will often plunge into depression as they try to wrap their mind and heart around what has happened. This is especially true if they do not have other grandchildren to console them and occupy their time or some other strong and consistent form of emotional support.

One ray of light and hope is the wonderful fact that there are several support groups available to grandparents who are estranged from their grandchildren. These group forums are heavily populated with good parents/grandparents who want nothing more than to love and be there for their children and grandchildren, but who, for whatever reason, find themselves on the outside looking in. To share and to see the commonality in stories is both a welcome relief and a balm to the heart. I cannot encourage you enough to take advantage of the many online support groups available to you. One way to find a support group is to simply type words in the search engine that are relevant to your particular situation.

The question of *WHY* this happens is a tricky one and almost always emotionally complicated. I will not pretend to be an expert, nor will I make the presumption that all adult children who make the decision *NOT* to allow their parents (grandparents) access to their children have done so out of immaturity, pettiness, spite, emotional illness, drug or alcohol addiction, or as some other form of parental retribution. I am absolutely sure there are wonderful parents out there, who because of their love for their children and their desire to keep them safe, have drawn healthy, and in some cases, necessarily stringent boundaries regarding access to their children. Parents/grandparents who were or are emotional or physical abusers, alcoholics, drug addicts, or who abandoned or neglected their own children (providing they have not profoundly changed and evolved) should be held in abeyance when it comes to their exposure to grandchildren. But again, I must ring out the battle cry—this book is not for or about those parents/grandparents; it was written for good parents and grandparents who have been emotionally abused, neglected, and lost in the fray.

Research and anecdotal statistics gleaned through dozens of interviews indicate that when there is an unhealthy relationship between mother and daughter, step-daughter and step-mother, or daughter-in-law and mother-in-law, that's when the sparks fly. According to research conducted in books, articles, interviews, and well-documented support-group data and statistics, somewhere in excess of 80% of all reported grandparent estrangement cases, as well as parent/adult-child estrangement cases involve female-on-female dynamics. Seldom was the isolation or abandonment initiated by a male family member. In short, almost every time the fire of family drama is ignited and then rages out of control, there's usually a woman stoking it.

As we've discussed, women, by our very nature, are highly competitive and territorial, even amongst friends. In fairness and to put that quality in a more flattering light, this quality is also what makes us amazing mothers. We own our job and become highly protective and territorial about our charge, and when that charge is a boyfriend, husband, and especially when it's a child, we become even more protective and territorial. These two qualities also make us fiercely competitive with anyone who encroaches on that territory; it's simply an intrinsic part of our nature. You don't have to ask a therapist for confirmation of that fact, simply observe women in competitive situations and scenarios and you'll see the internal power struggles play themselves out, in fact, merely being a member of the tribe, you will see and experience this side of femininity and its competitive edge first-hand. It's just that simple; no PHD necessary for that one.

Given that reality, if things aren't hunky dory between the alpha females as defined by their relationship to the charge (e.g., the loved-one they share in common), when and if grandchildren come along, they will invariably get stuck in the middle of the crossfire and can become pawns to one extent or another, just as children of divorce often do. Another component of this relationship dynamic is that many times, grandchildren are used as leverage over their grandparent(s). It happens all the time. I haven't met a grandparent yet who, to one degree or another, is not a member of that club.

It's just a question of whether they're gold or platinum members and what the nature and purpose for leveraging is. A loving and concerned adult-child might use the leverage of their parent's love for their grandchild as a means to motivate them to take better care of themselves so they'll be around longer for their beloved grandchild—that's a good thing! Then there is negative leveraging and the multiple ways it can be used to manipulate or control a grandparent. Some grandparents get off easy and only experience negative leveraging occasionally or in limited degrees while others are subjected to it regularly. Garnering financial enrichment, support, or childcare are often goals in manipulating and leveraging grandparents. When good grandparents are put through this hell, it is not only unacceptable but made worse by the fact that they have very few, if any rights, so if they want to see their grandchildren, they must take the hits if they want to play ball.

Cindy's Story

Cindy adored her three grandsons but had a troubled relationship with her daughter-in-law. It had been rocky from the beginning but Cindy had learned to roll with the punches. Her daughter-in-law would be friendly and inviting one week, then distant and hurtful the next, and always it seemed, without a catalyst or inciting event to provoke her. Cindy, as well as others close to her daughter-in-law often walked on egg shells around her, ever vigilant in their efforts not to invoke her fury. Time passed and Cindy eventually became somewhat conditioned to accept the times when, out of the blue, she would be deemed the enemy and tossed out of their lives. Cindy could see that it wasn't just her, it was other people too, so that made the pain more bearable. After being expelled, and being a devote super-pleaser/fixer/rescuer, Cindy's approach to the situation was to be more loving, more forgiving, and to try even harder to earn her way back into her daughter-in-law's good graces. Cindy's son seemed to no longer exist as either her son or as an individual entity. He did not take a stand one way or the other; he merely blew in whatever direction the wind (or his wife's wishes or whims) carried him. Her son had chosen, as many men do, the path of least resistance. (Don't forget the mathematical equation from chapter four.) The periods of estrangement would last anywhere from weeks to months and were total and complete. Cindy was always the one to offer an olive branch, be it a letter, card, call or perhaps a gift; she was constantly apologizing for one thing or another and always seeking earnestly to see her grandsons.

As the years went on the abuse grew worse and the periods of time that Cindy was estranged became longer and longer. Having bonded with her grandsons, the pain of separation was hard on Cindy. And although her pain was tremendous, knowing the confusion and pain that her grandsons must surely have felt caused an even deeper wound to Cindy's heart. Each time she would be invited back into the family, the children were a bit more skittish and stand-offish around their grandma. This hurt Cindy very deeply, but eventually she would win them over again. It was an exhausting exercise but well worth admission back into her family's good graces and grandson's hearts. But, without a doubt and as predictable as the seasons, the winter would come, and always unexpectedly; Cindy would return home from a visit and later receive a note or a call advising her that she was no longer welcome in their lives. On one occasion, Cindy was literally kicked out of the house in the middle of the night. Her son stoically drove his mother to the airport and dropped her off at the curb without so much as an explanation, hug, or a goodbye.

If this grandmother's story and her pain sound even remotely familiar, my heart goes out to you. Perhaps Cindy's story and the choices she was eventually forced to make can help you through your pain too.

After a decade of verbal abuse and emotional neglect coupled with intermittent, howbeit short-lived periods of civility, Cindy was again booted out, only this time something was different—the old girl (in her late sixties now) had lost her husband, survived cancer, was all alone in the world, and was now showing signs of emotional wear and tear; she was not holding up against the abuse and neglect as well as she used to. This time, when she got the boot, it was the last time. It was the last time because, it *had to be* the *last time* for her;

Cindy simply could not take it anymore, not mentally, physically, and not spiritually. Her grandsons were older now and with the passage of time and experiences shared together, her relationship with them was the one thing Cindy loved and cherished the most in life, and after her last ostracism from her only living family, Cindy plummeted, heart—first into major clinical depression. Even watching television would destroy her because inevitably she would see scenes in a movie, television show, or even commercials that depicted loving exchanges and embraces between a grandparent and their grandchild. It was more than she could bear.

Emotionally destitute and at a loss for any reason to continue living, Cindy sought counseling, and for the first time in her life, went on medication to manage the overwhelming depression and grief that had taken over her life as a result of again losing her grandsons. Therapy did offer useful insight into the troubled behavior of her daughter-in-law. As Cindy would later discover, her daughter-in-law had many troubled relationships, with the precarious one she shared with Cindy being just the tip of the iceberg. This news did not comfort or console Cindy, nor did it alleviate her pain or sense of profound loss; she was still emotionally devastated and stricken with despair. As a last ditch effort, Cindy joined a support group for grandparents who were estranged from their grandchildren and it helped immensely. The pain persisted but eventually Cindy's mood stabilized and she was able to stop taking medication to cope with her grief and loss, for that, she was grateful, but still, loneliness and heartache were never far away as she approached the prospect of never seeing her grandchildren again. Early-on in the on-going drama with her daughter-in-law, Cindy had been shocked and heartbroken when the gifts and cards she sent to her grandchildren during times of estrangement were returned the words *"unaccepted"*— *"denied"* or *"return to sender"* scribbled or sometimes stamped on the packages or envelops.

In her meditations and daily prayers for her son, daughter-in-law, and young grandsons, a unique idea occurred to Cindy, she would continue her communications with her grandsons in spite of being pushed out of the nest with the usual mandate that she *'never contact them again.'* Wanting to maintain contact and have the ability to express her love to the grandsons she missed so dearly, Cindy went to a craft store and bought three large trunks made of pine wood. She browsed about and found big wooden letters and selected the first initial for each of her grandson's names. This determined and inspired grandmother went through all the miscellaneous wooden decorations that could be glued onto the trunks and selected designs she knew each boy would love. With the back of her old station wagon filled to the brim, she drove home, and over the course of the next week, Cindy prayerfully and loving decorated each trunk for her three grandsons. When they were done, it was a bittersweet moment for Cindy as she looked at the finely decorated trunks. For a brief moment she recoiled in sadness at the idea of their necessity, but quickly regained her composure and joy. Cindy relished the *gift* of being about to do something for her grandsons and for herself too. Cindy had created a connection to her grandsons, one that no one would take away from her. It was very powerful, and out of a profound pain mingled with an enduring love, this grandmother had created her own means of maintaining love and connection to her grandchildren.

Things did not get better for Cindy and over the painful years that followed, whenever she felt the ache in her heart of missing her grandsons, or whenever she wanted to talk them, hold them, or simply say *'grandma loves you,'* Cindy would date and write a letter, get a card or a little gift and tuck it away in the trunks. This thoughtful grandmother created a ritual for herself and her grandsons and has managed to keep the faith that one day, even if they're adults, her grandsons will have an opportunity to open their special trunks and see all the photos, notes, cards, crafts, gifts and keepsakes their grandma made and gave to them over the years. They will know that they were never far from her thoughts and always in her heart. One day, near or far off, those precious boys would know they were loved dearly by their grandma, even if she wasn't around to see that day or share the experience with them. Although nothing could replace actually being present in her grandson's lives, Cindy was now empowered and her burden lightened by maintaining contact and connection with her beloved grandsons via her rituals, and she did it on her own terms. Cindy continues that ritual to this day.

What does estrangement do to grandchildren?

I am not a psychologist or psychiatrist; I'm just your average human being who happens to also be a mother and a grandmother, just like you. I have, however, devoted a large part of my life to my own on-going education and personal growth, and consequently, am very well read on the subject of family and inter-personal relationships, and have performed a great deal of research and interviewing of regular parents just like myself. That, combined with the real life stories so courageously shared with me, as well as from my own life experiences, gives me solid ground to stand on when I tell you, both as a parent and layperson whose been in the trenches, the emotional pain and confusion that grandchildren suffer when an emotionally healthy, loving grandparent is yanked out of their life is as intense and immeasurable as is the damage done to their precious little hearts and minds. I have witnessed the damage firsthand and can tell you—it is one of the most irrational, confusing, cruel, and destructive of all dysfunctional family dynamics I've encountered. Grandparents are supposed to be tried and true Rocks of Gibraltar for their grandchildren and when good grandparents disappear from the landscape of a child's life and it happens within the space of an emotional whim or fire-storm or because a troubled or territorial parent is using them as leverage, to act-out, or to punish their own parents, it is absolutely confounding and devastating to the innocent children involved. Grandchildren are not capable of understanding what is happening or why; that makes the actions of their parents incredibly selfish, unhealthy, and destructive. You don't need a degree to know that, just a beating heart and a healthy conscience. It is the total destruction of innocence and trust that occurs when a grandchild is used in this way that is most heartbreaking of all.

In a world where unthinkable/unimaginable disasters, catastrophes, and crimes are occurring on a daily basis, and sometimes in their own neighborhoods and communities, children are already exposed to so much risk and daily stresses, it is hard to imagine what life is like for small, impressionable children today, but to then intentionally add unnecessary confusion, stress, and pain, seems to me to be a cruelty beyond explanation or justification, especially when it is doled out by a child's own parent.

It reminds me of what will become this book's reframe

Love is not a test; nor is it a competition or a game to be won or lost or a war to be waged. Love cannot be won or lost, only shared. No person or love itself should be defined or held as property; it cannot be owned and must never be lorded over, hoarded, or hidden away and not shared. Love is a gift—a blessing! Love is an inheritance our children and our children's children should have every right to and assurance of. Foremost, love has the incredible ability to manifest where once there was none; it can multiply and is eternal and endless. That means there is more than enough to go around and to share. We would all do well to remind ourselves of that daily.

---

* Note: there are instances when grandparents actually sue to gain grandparents rights. It is beyond the scope or intent of this book to investigate that subject; however, we do want good, well-intended grandparents to know that in some states, and when deemed appropriate, that has been a successful course of action for grandparents who wish to see their grandchildren.

CHAPTER 12

The Haunting Question—
What Did I Do Wrong?

Making Yourself Responsible & Wrong

Has your life become a dump site for guilt or other toxic emotional waste?

In addition to worrying obsessively, and always trying to please or meet a need, we mothers are also notorious for taking the blame. Crazy as it sounds, when it comes to our kids, we'll throw ourselves in front of the bus, take the bullet, beat ourselves up and many times we allow our children to join in or even be the ring-leader. In addition to being the most rewarding of vocations in life, motherhood can also be a call to hazardous duty too; it definitely not a job for the easily wearied or faint of heart. However, having said that, ironically, sometimes the very selfless nature that makes us awesome moms to start off with changes dramatically as the years roll by, and what was once a vibrant, confident, giving woman and mother is transformed into a helpless victim. That is why mothers who don't grow and expand as individuals along with their children are so adept at becoming martyrs and victims to the cause. But remember—there are no victims, only volunteers, and just as they fully embraced and embodied the role of mother, sometimes to the exclusion of everything else, these mothers fully embody the role of victim. This includes taking on the burden of making yourself wrong, blaming yourself, and keeping yourself immersed in the emotions and baggage that all this drama carries with it. I say this because I've seen it happen so many times and because I have walked this painful path myself and can tell you—it is a vast wasteland where virtually nothing but pain and loss can grow.

Why do we end up here? How does it happen?

It usually sets in when your children begin pushing against the boundaries of early childhood. Where once you were your child's *all* and *everything* in virtually every imaginable way, and exercised loving dominion over them, over time, your supreme role as mother, guardian, authority figure, super hero, savior, provider, and master of their universe begins to fade as they begin to cut the apron strings. And if you're like most moms, you felt vacant when your child's attachment to and need for those old roles was challenged and eventually overthrown. There was a *coup d'etat* and no one told you. This can be overwhelming, even devastating to moms who tenaciously cling to their role of supreme gatekeeper and demy-god to their child. Especially at risk are mothers who continue to make their children their principal reason for living and the primary, if not singular source of their identity. I certainly was guilty as charged, and you may be too. Just understand that although this does not excuse the subsequent unacceptable behaviors that accompany this role reversal, it does place a certain amount of ownous on you. Parents who lost control and became super-pleasers and over-indulged their children, admitted that at some point they became the needy one, the empty hole that needed filling, and it was at that moment that a shift in power took place.

You can't respect someone who doesn't respect themselves.

So, what do we do? Here's the short answer—if you've done wrong, and by wrong, I mean, if you set up your relationship so that your children were there to meet *your* emotional needs, fill *you up* and sustain *you*, then obviously that pattern needs to be broken. Why must it be broken? Because, by clinging desperately to a stage of motherhood you should have evolved past long ago, you made a mistake that has, at best stifled the relationship you have with your adult-child and has made you a steaming hot pile of neediness and pain. By continuing to get your needs met, or trying to get your needs met in that way, you have immersed yourself in the classic victim archetype. You do this by wanting/needing the quality of love and validation you once received from your child when they were very young and totally dependent upon you. It becomes a vicious cycle as the pain continues, it drives your sense of loss which then feeds into an increased sense of neediness, as that neediness increases so does your child's adverse response to your weakness, this produces more pain and the cycle starts all over again. And all the while, you blame either yourself or your child for your life conditions, level of unhappiness or lack of fulfillment.

The end result of this vicious cycle is the total assumption of the victim role as you bounce off your E-generation child's ever increasing abrasive or neglectful behavior. You may even subconsciously provoke negative situations or responses in order to get attention or complete and validate your victim role. Positive or negative, there's still a huge emotional pay-off in it for you and it keeps you *involved* in your adult child's life, even if it's in a negative context. When we take a brutally honest look at ourselves, it is fair to say that in many instances we (me and you) are, at the very least, complicit in our own fate and current state of unhappiness. Maybe you clung to your kids for your emotional support and nourishment when you should have been depending on yourself; and maybe you gave your kids all your love but also expected them to fill you up in return, and when they didn't or couldn't do that for you anymore, you lost your identity and sank into the role of helpless victim. Can you see how the melodrama begins and how it keeps spinning and playing itself out in a vicious cycle? I hope so, because if you can see that, then you will be open to creating a place where it can end; a place where you can experience healing, growth, and a new beginning. A place where you can create and emanate the love you crave rather than waiting for someone else to do it for you. No one can fill you up and then keep you topped-off emotionally except for *you.*

I recall my own mother being a master at embodying the victim role in her life and then playing it out in the lives of those around her. She constantly reminded me of all she had done for her children and what she had given up in order to be a mother. *"I did this for you and I sacrificed that for you."* It seemed as if I could never be grateful enough to fill her up sufficient to feel assured of my love and appreciation. My mother had a big beautiful heart, but inside that incredible heart was a hole that no human being could fill, try as they may. The only person that could make her feel whole, loved, and worthy was *her*, but sadly, my mother didn't know that, and it was the *not knowing* that made her a very needy soul who never felt the joy of self fulfillment or healthy, authentic love. The lesson I took from my early years was that making a full-grown adult feel loved and valued as a human being is a tall order for anyone, let alone a kid. It's also something we would do well to remember as mothers.

What you can do for yourself and ultimately for your child, regardless of their age, is take an honest inventory of your life. Look deep inside and identify what role you have either voluntarily assumed or have been assigned in this melodrama entitled: *'My Relationship with My Adult Child.'* After you acknowledge where you're at in the car or on the highway, identify the behaviors and patterns that are keeping you stuck there. Once you have done that, you must commit to giving up the victim role and its inherent emotional pay offs, that means the pity parties, as gratifying as they may seem, and as many of your base emotional needs as they may temporarily meet, MUST GO. Stop wearing your pain and your role as abandoned, neglected parent as a kind of badge of honor, or more appropriately, as a badge of pity and victimhood and instead, start believing and appreciating that you do not need to make yourself wrong, take the blame, or be a victim anymore. It's all up to you. But whatever you do, you cannot expect the change to start with your kids. No matter their age, growth and transformation *must* start with *you* deciding that living in a wasteland is no longer acceptable and that you do not deserve it and will no longer tolerate it, not one minute longer. And remember—this is your life and happiness we're talking about mom, so take charge of it or I assure you, someone else will.

CHAPTER 13

When to *'Just Say <u>NO</u>'*

Setting Healthy Boundaries
Under Trying Circumstances

Saying *no,* even under the best of circumstances can be difficult for many parents to do. This is certainly true of moms, and especially true of needy, codependent moms. And if it's true under the best of circumstances, then one can only imagine the strength, confidence, and sheer guts it takes for a parent to stand in love and say no when the circumstances are difficult and challenging.

When alcohol or drug addiction is the issue

Alcohol has become such an accepted social lubricant in our culture that it sounds rather puritanical to speak of it in the negative. After all, what would Super Bowl Sunday or New Year's Eve be without alcohol paving the way for all the fun and celebration, right? In addition to that accepted social standard, most children grow up with parents/role models who readily, and in many cases daily demonstrate that drinking is as much a part of one's daily rituals as brushing one's teeth in the morning, going to work, or picking up a fork to eat with; drinking has become a part of our national identity and routine.

What about teens and adult-children who drink? Where do we stand there as a nation?

According to the National Institute on Alcohol Abuse and Alcoholism—*"An overwhelming majority of college students (88%) including those under the legal drinking age, have used alcohol . . ."* Many of the students polled admitted that during their college years, the regular consumption of alcohol was not only encouraged, it was expected. Most shocking, of those surveyed, 60-70% indicated that they had developed some kind of drinking *'issue'* after leaving college, even if labeled *'social or binge drinking.'* So what's a parent to do? First and foremost, it's hard to throw rocks when you live in a glass house. The old adage of *"Do as I tell you, not as I do"* no longer applies. You can't smoke like a chimney or drink like a fish and then judge, ridicule, or discipline your child for faithfully following in your footsteps when they reach their teen years or adulthood. If you are <u>not</u> *'that parent'* but find yourself battling with a child who is abusing alcohol or drugs, the first thing you need to grasp is the fact that meaningful, committed intervention and rehab are essential. Ignoring a problem and hoping it will go away on its own is not the answer and doesn't work. Remember, we cannot change what we do not acknowledge and confront. If your attempts to intervene and/or rehab has been repeatedly rejected or the abuse and disease have accelerated to a level where crime or abuse is occurring, then you must answer the ultimate tough-love question: *Does there come a time when enough is enough?* If so, when is enough, enough? Have things reached a point of no return? Is there a point when a parent has no alternative but to toss up their hands, throw in the towel and concede defeat? That is a very personal question and is unique to each family, their social/economic situation, as well as the attitudes and behaviors of the teen or adult-child involved. I have known and have interviewed parents who have been successful in employing an intervention, and I've met those that have failed miserably, even after numerous attempts at intervention and rehab. I have heard the sorrowful cries of parents who have lost everything of monetary value in their lives in order to provide their adult child with repeat trips to rehab, only to ultimately watch helplessly as their child succumbed to their addiction.

Devastated parents have shared their heartache and their stories with me. Parents who have had their valuables stolen by a drug addicted child; parents who have witnessed their children selling themselves on street corners for drugs; parents who have bailed their children out of jail so many times, they lost count, as well as stories of well-meaning parents who have spent their very last dime putting their adult-child through rehab for the third or fourth time, to no avail, and are now broke. The truth is—we can love them, pray for them, make every effort to help them get well, but we cannot make them *want to* or do it for them. We can *want it for them* but we cannot do it for them or force it upon them. Until and unless the addicted person/adult child wants to get clean and stay clean, they won't do it and the painful truth is: there is precious little we can do to effect healing and recovery, that is something they must do for themselves.

One mother I interviewed had mortgaged away her home in order to pay for multiple trips to rehab, none of which were successful. Ultimately this loving single parent lost her home and their daughter succumbed to her addiction in spite of all the love and effort extolled on the part of her mother. So what can we take from such a tragic story? When is enough, enough? Is there never an end to a parent's obligation to be there for, care for, and rescue their child? What is the answer? Some of you may be upset that the question is even being asked. For other parents, the answer may be a resounding YES—there does come a time to stop; a time to just say *"no more!"* For others, there will never come a point at which they will lose hope or give up. There is no easy answer and it's different for each parent. Certainly if a parent has the means by which to send their adult child to rehab, and they (the adult child) are willing to go and are committed to their own recovery, then by all means, I don't think wild horses could keep a parent from making that financial investment in their child. But, what about the parents who simply cannot afford it or whose adult child defies all attempts to help them? Statistics suggest that these financially beleaguered parents comprise the majority of our population; they are the ones for whom an all-expense-paid trip to rehab is simply not possible. What if one's adult child does not want to get well and rejects the help? What then?

How does the parent cope? Remember this book is meant to support *you*, the parents, not the users. If you don't have the money but are committed to helping and believe your child is just as committed to their recovery as you are, there are low-cost rehab facilities, as well as county and state-run programs available.

★Check with your community's local law enforcement, social services, and/ or Health department, as well as local churches, community groups, and Free Clinics.

What if you've endured years of abuse, lying, stealing, mooching, and all that comes with alcohol or drug addiction? First, if you have been an enabler to your child's addiction that must STOP immediately. If you're in danger or being abused, you must make a decision as to whose welfare is paramount; is it yours, any innocent grandchildren or grandparents that may be involved? Or is it your adult child's? You are not doing anyone, especially yourself or your addicted child any favors by allowing them to either use or abuse you or your home. Whether or not you elect to be a cheerleader and supporter for your child, you must take care of yourself and other dependent family members first. Remember, you are no good to anyone if you're not taking good care of yourself.

Silvia's Story

Silvia's daughter Carrie became addicted to drugs in her teens. Her mother, a devout Catholic, had laid down the law but it was patently ignored. Silvia went to Mass, prayed the rosary, and hoped for the best. The drug abuse continued, eventually becoming so bad that Carrie regularly stole from her mothers' purse in order to pay for her habit. One day, desperate for drugs, Carrie raided her mother's jewelry box and stole all her antique jewelry, including family heirlooms that had been passed down and entrusted to many generations of Silvia's family. In addition to stealing from her mother, Carrie would run away from home on a regular basis. Silvia would spend nights driving through the seedy areas of Newark looking for her only-daughter on street corners and outside flop houses. She would put herself at risk each time she rescued her daughter and brought her home, and each time, within days, something valuable would disappear along with Carrie. After an argument escalated to the boiling point and Silvia was struck by her daughter as she pled for her not to leave, she was done! Silvia did not look for her daughter nor did she want her back in her house. She had hit her limit, or so she thought.

Months went by with no word. Finally, alone, hungry, and desperate for a place to stay, Carrie eventually made her way home and under the condition that her daughter *get clean*, Silvia accepted her with open arms. All was well for six weeks; however, by the end of the second month, Carrie was again using drugs. She was also up to her old behaviors, but this time, to Carrie's shock and dismay, her mother called the police and had her daughter, who was now 18, removed from her home. The young woman was indignant but *this time* mom had made her mind up, it was over, and this time, for good; Silvia could no longer tolerate the drama in her life. That was over five years ago, and although her daughter, still drug addicted and living on the streets, has reached out to her, Silvia has not responded; for this mother, once the door shut for the last time, it was closed forever.

Some may find the finality of Silvia's decision harsh. I do not believe anyone can judge another parents decision(s) relative to what is ultimately best for either them or their adult children. We are placed on this earth to live and experience our lives fully and to (hopefully) learn what it is we're meant to learn from our experiences. We share our lives with others—our family, friends, colleagues, acquaintances, and even the strangers we meet, but at the end of the day, we wake up and go to sleep with only one person, ourselves. Therefore, we can only make decisions and commitments on behalf of ourselves. And when it's all said and done, we are responsible for only ourselves and what we do with our life. So the truth is this, as much as we as parents may want to, we cannot make life choices for our adult children, and seldom are we imbued with enough power to revoke or reverse the bad decisions our adult children may elect to make. We may try with all our might to influence or change others (and we often do) but ultimately, it is *their life* to live and *their choice* alone to make (or not make). At the end of the day and at the end of our lives, we are, each of us, only responsible for our own individual beliefs, behaviors, choices, and lifestyle. We can love and be a positive influence in the lives of others and I'll list some of those things below, but what our loved ones ultimately do, or do not do with their life is entirely their choice and their choice alone.

Some things you can do

- ❖ Love your children and educate them when they are young and impressionable.
- ❖ Set not just a good, but an *exemplary standard* for them to trust in and follow.
- ❖ Be consistent in your standards, commitments, and goals.
- ❖ Do not lie or be a hypocrite; your children will disrespect and mistrust you for it and later rebel against your hypocrisy and false standards.
- ❖ Let them know when they've fallen down, help them up, educate them, and support them when it's appropriate to do so.
- ❖ Love them tenaciously, but love yourself also, and with just as much tenacity.
- ❖ Establish healthy/reasonable boundaries and standards to live by and maintain them lovingly.
- ❖ Intervene if you can, if you cannot, release them with love and pray for them and their physical and ultimately spiritual healing.

When personality or social disorders /mental illness is an Issue

This is a topic that is seldom spoken about because it's a sensitive subject and is as individual to each person and their life circumstances as one's finger prints. I have interviewed parents whose adult children are schizophrenic, bi-polar, severely narcissistic or suffer with personality dysfunctions such as anti-social disorder, borderline personality disorder, etc. In each instance, the parent involved suffers indescribable fear, worry, pain, and loss, as well as verbal/emotional torment and abuse in some cases. Of the dozen of mothers and fathers interviewed, all of them said that they love their adult-child dearly but that when the behaviors got out of control or dangerous, they had to get outside help, hospitalize their child, or if the child was living independently, withdraw themselves from the madness in order to keep themselves sane. This is particularly true when the adult child is not compliant with health and lifestyle requirements (i.e., abstinence from alcohol and/or drugs, refusal to take prescribed meds, etc.) or if they had become hostile or violent.

We will not go into detail about each of these disorders, as each of them deserve an entire chapter (even books) of their own and I am not qualified to properly analyze or elaborate on them. However, I do encourage you to seek out an expert and do your own research. Most important of all, find a support group to join. This is essential because if you are a parent whose adult child suffers from an emotional condition, disorder, or mental illness, you are painfully aware of the challenges that face you on a daily (sometimes hourly) basis, particularly if the adult child is not aware of their condition or willing to accept help, and especially if there are grandchildren involved. If your child is committed to getting as healthy as they possibly can and to seeking the help they need, then of course, it's a parent's duty and privilege to be there for their child; however, it's been my observation that, that is often not the case. Often, parents suffer estrangement from their adult-child not because they want to or initiate it but because their adult child chooses it, or more precisely, their adult-child's illness controls their behavior and therefore dictates their actions. This includes hostility towards and estrangement from loved ones. As heartbreaking as this reality is, it is still not reason enough for a loving parent to be tormented, abused or violated.

Mental illness is a selfish and insidious theft that steals away a person's ability to make reasonable, well-thought-out, clear choices in their life. Every day it robs and destroys families in this country. For those parents, mothers, and grandparents who have their hearts broken regularly as a result of personality disorders/mental illness and its many faces and manifestations, I again implore you to join a support group. Learn to take care of yourself, and if it feels right, incorporate some of the techniques Cindy used to keep sadness and depression at bay and help maintain a sense of contact and connection with your adult child or grandchildren.

When an independent adult-child chooses *not* to seek help or be compliant with their medication, therapy, or lifestyle mandates, and uses their parents as rescuers, ATMs, emotional or literal punching bags or routinely kicks them to the curb in order to satisfy some internal need to punish or act out, the parents need to lovingly establish healthy boundaries. In addition to caring about/for their sick child, they must also care for themselves, any grandchildren involved, as well as their child's ultimate well being. They do that by no longer acting as an enabler to their adult child's disease. They do that by no longer permitting or rationalizing away the dangerous behavior, abuse, emotional abandonment and/or stress and drama they are experiencing.

And what if you just don't like the person your adult-child has become?

It would be naïve and unrealistic to write a book about the triumphs, trials and tribulations of being a parent and all the pit-falls along the way, if we're not willing recognize the dark side of parenting too. We must address the painful fact that sometimes, in spite of our best efforts, there will be a few kids that grow up to be inconsiderate, self-absorbed, thoroughly shallow and materialistic narcissists who don't have time for anyone but themselves. In spite of a parent's best efforts, there are also those that grow into amoral, anti-social criminals or lazy social/familial parasites who think everybody owes them something in life. There! I said it. Hell, someone had to. If that happens, we must accept that ultimately, all children grow up to be their *own person*. They develop their own interests and peer groups, and sadly, sometimes, their lifestyle and core values (or lack thereof) are the polar opposite of those modeled by and anticipated by their parents. That is why I believe it is possible to love your adult-child but to also quite objectively *not like them* as a person. How many of you have a sibling or other relative that you love (because they're 'family') but frankly, if you met them on the street, you'd keep walking? The same relationship dynamics can exist between parents and their teenager or adult child. It is the societal rules and expectations surrounding *family* that keep us bound in unhealthy relationships and situations, even when the most abusive, painful, and damaging relationships we have are within our own family.

Speculating on family dynamics and intra-family relationships that are unhealthy, yet are rigorously maintained nonetheless, Samuel Butler, a Cambridge graduate, author, philosopher, and member of the clergy wrote:

"I believe more unhappiness comes from this source (family) than any other—I mean the attempt to prolong family connection unduly, and to make people hang together artificially who would never naturally do so."

Key in Mr. Butler's statement is the word *"unduly."* If healthy love and family harmony are gone, if respect is nonexistent, and if abuse or distain have replaced family love and bonding, then I believe Samuel Butler's words ring out loudly that we should examine the health of our relations, even those within our own family. When it comes to our kids, love can never be lost or entirely evicted from our hearts, but rapport, respect, and simply likeability can most certainly wane or deteriorate all together. In those instances, the best decision may very well be to release that family member and love them from a safe and sane distance, at least until a safe, healthy, and mutually loving and respectful relationship is possible.

CHAPTER 14

What Healthy Love Is & What it is Not

A mother's love is an unrelenting, incredibly powerful force that is almost impossible to define in terms other than those only another mother can understand. I am also of the belief that unless you've experienced motherhood, you can never fully understand what it means to truly and selflessly love another human being the way mothers love their children. We carry them in our wombs, we see them through birth, and for some mothers through harrowing complications that arise after. We nurse our babies and we wear the scars of both our love and our journey on our bodies for life. There are also those special souls who are mothers and fathers of choice; they're the ones who perhaps went through years of waiting and bureaucratic red tape in order to adopt their child.

As all good mothers will tell you, there is absolutely nothing we won't do for our children. We would die for them without hesitation, in a heartbeat, in fact and in actuality, we do that every day as a mother. Whether it's sacrificing our own wants and needs for our child by making sure they get that outfit or dress they want, the doll, train set, or video game, or the new-cool tennis shoes they absolutely *must have*. We've spent years and years making it our supreme purpose to be there for them when they're happy, sad, sick, or scared. No matter what, we moms are on the job. We dutifully fulfill the roles of comforter, maid, cook, nursemaid, playmate, teacher, personal valet, philosopher, chauffeur, and personal financier. We never tire of sacrificing for them, putting them first, and fulfilling their needs and desires as best we can. And in those rare private moments before exhaustion and sleep overtake us, our last thoughts are of them and their welfare. It's just what we moms do. But here's a controversial question—is loving our children to the near or total exclusion of everything and everyone else, including ourselves, really what's best for us as women or for our children?

The women I spoke with while writing this book fell into two separate and distinct groups. There were those that love and adore their children but who have always maintained their own personal life and identity independent of their children and are sure to make time for that private life, as well as for the other significant people in their life. They were the moms who established boundaries and goals relative to what kinds of behavior they expected from their children, as well as what behaviors their children could expect and rely upon from them. They also established what behaviors and attitudes were unacceptable and would not be tolerated early on. They were sure to let their children know that there were absolutes in the relationship *(i.e., things they, as mothers would not do for them)*. At first glance that sounds harsh, especially if you're a big marshmallow or pushover like so many of us moms. But, with the benefit of time and hindsight, it can be confidently said that later in life these wise mothers experienced far more autonomy relative to their relationship with their adult child. They also enjoyed a mutual love and respect that was healthy and enriching for both parties.

So how about the rest of us—the *other* moms? You know who you are and that's why you bought this book. Don't feel bad. You are definitely not alone. Beyond that, take comfort in knowing that it appears that you are actually in the majority (at least according to my research, interviews, and surveys). So what do you think defines the second group of mothers? The second group was comprised of women who, like myself, often grew up being told by their mothers, fathers, and society that their primary goal in life was to *get married and raise kids*. In retrospect, it's pretty crazy to consider that there was a time in this country's cultural history when little girls were not encouraged to be whatever they wanted to be when they grew up. Centuries of social conditioning, social boundaries and glass ceilings were firmly in place and appeared impervious. We were not encouraged to be independent women who may or may not desire the role of wife and mother; rather, it was a time when the mere idea of growing up to be a doctor, attorney or engineer was sheer science fiction. If we were *'not the marrying kind'* (didn't fit a man's ideal of the model wife), we were labeled spinsters and were encouraged to become teachers, secretaries, bank tellers (a clerical job in those days) or join a typing pool (yes, such a thing actually existed). If a woman was really smart or inspired, she became a nurse; precious few became doctors. According to Project Muse—Today's Research/ Tomorrow's Inspiration—*"For nearly a century, clerical work has been the archetypal paid job for women in North America. Initially dominated by men, clerical occupations quickly became among the most gender-segregated of all jobs: numerically dominated by women and discursively marked as 'women's work'."*

Most female baby boomers grew up being told over and over again that they needed to find a good man to take care of them, and thereafter, be a good wife and mother. And after the single-most defining event of their life-marriage, they carried out their duties obediently and faithfully. They cooked, cleaned, sewed, and stayed at home and tended to the house and kids. As young girls, if there was any doubt as to our destiny, our duties became more clearly defined once we entered junior high school, where a class was offered exclusively for us budding young brides-to-be. Instruction took place in a *'girls only'* classroom/a kitchen where we would learn to cook, clean, and sew. The official name of the class was HOME ECONOMICS and it was a required course. For those of us who accepted this as our station in life, our supreme purpose and identity, our high calling in life, we immersed ourselves in our role as wife and mother with absolute devotion and never dreamt of cultivating another life purpose or identity. Even our wedding vows contained a pledge to love, honor, and *obey* our husbands, and when the minister, priest or judge would conclude the ceremony, it almost always ended with—*'I now pronounce you man and wife'*—never husband and wife. The man remained a man but the woman had become a *'wife.'* In those days, to challenge the man of the house, society, or the old paradigm was not just discouraged and frowned upon, it was deemed either an irrationally selfish act or a fit of pure insanity, and in some quarters, a sin. That's why most of us *good girls* bought into it hook, line, and sinker.

For those of us who fall into the latter group, we were taught to serve and love our families unconditionally. We were not brought up to have a sense of identity outside of our role as wife and mother. Most of us were trained to give and keep giving and never set boundaries around other people's treatment of us. Hell, we couldn't own our own property until the mid 70's, prior to that, if a woman owned property in her own name in some states, it automatically conveyed over to her husband upon marriage. In short, we were literally and legally considered chattel (i.e., property, such as a slave). Our very identity and existence was dependent upon maintaining our role of wife and mother, and that is how many of us solely defined ourselves; we didn't know any better. Later, because of our one-dimensional identity, as our children grow older and begin to pull away, we cling all the more. Any semblance of power we may have possessed in the past gives way to our neediness, and our kids know it. That's when most of us try to become *friends* or submissively become super pleasers/servers/fixers/rescuers. That's also when abuses are likely to occur (verbal, emotional, financial); and what do we do? When this power shift occurs, it's because we have either consciously or subconsciously invited and/or encouraged it. We do this because in our hearts, we rationalize that if we do, our kids will know that we love them unconditionally; and if they know how much we love them, surely they will then recognize that they love and still need us just as badly as we need to be needed by them. And if they love and need us, then we get to maintain our sense of identity, value, and purpose. After all, weren't we taught that wife and/or mother was our primary role, function, and purpose for living. See how that works.

What all this means is—if your children become your entire life, your entire identity, your primary purpose for living and only source of love and validation in your life, you're in for a roller coaster ride of emotions. And although we have said a lot about the E-generation and how they are more likely to take advantage of, and have higher expectations of their parents, as well as what they believe they're *owed* by either society or their parents, that does not let you off the hook mom; it only aggravates the problem. If you've made your children your primary or singular source of love, identity, purpose, and validation, then you have placed a heavy burden on your child that is not theirs to carry. You've also set both them and yourself up to fail in parent/child relations because once you become *'that needy'* and have no sense of *self* to draw strength from, you become an emotional parasite, and like all parasites, you will be seen as a pest and eventually brushed off or even squashed if you become too much of an irritant. You will always love your child—that's how you're built, but if you channel some of your energies into finding out *who you are* and *what makes 'you' happy,* you will change your entire world. In addition to that, you'll be a better parent for it. In other words, when you focus on *'getting a life'* and letting your kids *live their own life,* you will gain insights, grow dramatically, and become a happier, more centered, and stronger person. You will be the respected and respectable person you so long to be. You will develop a tremendous level of self confidence, and will as a result, become worthy of the respect you may have sacrificed to your children in order to get your emotional needs met.

In the end, we moms love fiercely and forever. We can also be wounded and have our hearts broken by our children. What I think is important to remember is that love takes on many disguises in life and manifests in many ways and forms. Sometimes, what may feel is an act of *loving our child* is not, and what is hard, if not impossible to do, and is the thing our child detests the most, may, in the end, be the most selfless and profound act of love on our part, even when it's hard to execute. What is true is that love that is not deeply rooted in and exemplified by honesty and mutual respect is not a healthy or abiding love. We must take on the challenge to love ourselves and our children while maintaining healthy/respectful boundaries.

- ❖ You must love and respect yourself.
- ❖ You must have or develop your own identity and core values.
- ❖ You must possess your own purpose in life.

When you accomplish that, your life becomes independent, strong, enriched and enriching to others. That's when you have something to offer to your children rather than continuing to play the role of servant to them. When you respect yourself, others will respect you too, including your children.

Now . . .

- ❖ Imagine developing your own interests and purpose in life.
- ❖ Imagine a life where you are in control, self-expressed, and confident.
- ❖ Imagine learning to love yourself first, so you can love others from that healthy place.
- ❖ Imagine respecting yourself, so you can respect others from that same healthy place.
- ❖ Imagine valuing yourself the way you value your children.
- ❖ Imagine becoming a strong, independent woman.
- ❖ Imagine becoming a colorful, fascinating, and intensely interesting woman.
- ❖ Imagine inspiring others including your children with your character, integrity, strength, and the vibrant quality of your life.

CHAPTER 15

The Danger of Making Your Child Your Primary Reason for Living

&

Why it's not Healthy for Them, and Especially not for You

At first glance, this may sound counter-intuitive and even insulting to mothers, especially mothers of younger children but it is the truth. The more we lose ourselves, our individuality, our independence, and our identity by becoming our child's total servant (in an unhealthy way with few or no boundaries) and they, our masters or perhaps even dictators, the less respect we have for and of ourselves, and the less respect our children will ultimately have for us.

In some pack groups, what happens to the most vulnerable and frail member of a herd? They can't keep up, fall behind and are lost or killed-off because they are the weakest and easiest member of the pack to lose or sacrifice. In some family groups, many loving, well-meaning mothers have been emotionally killed-off, and ironically, it was their obsessive and sometimes suffocating need to love, serve, save, and be ever-ready and ever-present that ultimately spelled their doom. Mothers like this are often referred to as *Smother Mothers*. Bottomless pit syndrome drove them to relentlessly seek the acceptance and approval they so desperately need from their children in order to feel loved, validated, and whole. That neediness and what they're willing to do to fill the void is what these women call devote or unconditional love but is ultimately not an act of love and does

130

not instill or ensure love, but rather, becomes their undoing. It is also these self-effacing/self-sacrificing mothers who suffer the worst with empty nest syndrome years down the road and the reasons are not hard to identify. Again, we're not talking about well-balanced motherhood; we're talking about mothers who lose themselves entirely, who cater to lazy, helpless or demanding, misbehaving, and often disrespectful or unappreciative children rather than parenting them properly by demonstrating healthy love via setting growth/respect oriented boundaries around your and their behavior.

To authentically love your child is to be committed to their growth and development as a caring, responsible, empathic human being.

All good mothers give effortlessly and selflessly of themselves and it's an admirable quality. In fact, it's so admirable that God/the Universe/Nature in its infinite wisdom decided we were the best qualified of the species to carry, bear, nurture, and raise newborn infants into adulthood. No wonder, Tenneva Jordan, when speaking of a mother's selfless love, wrote: *"A mother is a person who seeing there are only four pieces of pie for five people, promptly announces (that) she never did care for pie."* I'm sure that adage rings true for many of us; however, there does come a point in each mother's life when she must (for her health and that of her children) become autonomous, get acquainted with her individuality and begin living life for herself and on her own terms. As admirable as *selfless love* may be, healthy maternal love is not what is at issue here. It is when that love becomes an obsessive personal *need* that problems arise. When children become the ultimate and singular source of love, gratification, and identity for a woman/mother, that is when the seeds of potentially serious problems and pain are planted. This happens when a woman's sense of *self* is lost; when she places herself and her intimate relationship *after* the children; when her sole purpose in life is to please and serve, and by that function seek (and hopefully receive) approval and acceptance from her primary source of fulfillment—her children. When that kind of shift occurs in mothering, the entire parent/child infrastructure collapses and a new environment and social order is established, a new government if you will, and this new government can easily become a dictatorship;

a place where no one wins and mom becomes the ultimate martyr to the cause.

Why we put kids first

Lynn was a woman who had been repeatedly hurt in life and as a consequence did not trust men. As a result of her emotional scars and mistrust, Lynn placed all her emotional stock in her children. In a very basic sense, she put all her eggs in one basket and then bet the farm on it. Lynn thought that by loving her kids and giving unselfishly to them excessively and to a fault, that they would behave in kind and treat her with the same level of unconditional love and singularly focused devotion she had demonstrated toward them over the years. Lynn, like so many mothers, was wrong. *(More about Lynn a little later)*

An Odd Dichotomy

When asked the question—Who comes first in your life, yourself, your husband or your children? What is your priority? Without a moment's hesitation, a whooping nine out of ten mothers interviewed immediately and enthusiastically replied that their children were the most important person(s) or priority in their life. That struck me as being an incredible statistic, so I double-checked the data; I asked ten more mothers, and this time, seven out of ten said their children were the most important person/priority in their life including one that waffled. With statistics like this, it's no wonder the divorce rate is so high in this country. Incidentally, the same mothers who said their children come before all others, also ranked their children as being more important than their own emotional, social, financial, physical or psychological health and welfare. It's hard to know whether these mothers are to be commended or committed when one considers their absolute blind devotion to their children, particularly if that devotion trumps everything and everyone else in their life.

Although at first glance, all this love and self-sacrifice sounds very endearing and commendable, it can ultimately become a very selfish/self-destructive way of living. Interviews and anecdotal research have revealed that these same women are more likely to be divorced one or more times, feel under-loved, under-appreciated, and ultimately unacknowledged by their children as they grow older and more independent. They also did not possess a strong sense of an *independent self.* In an odd paradox, the women who were identified as attentive smother mothers also suffered with bouts of resentment toward their adult children, as well as anxiety and/or depression.

Note: The average age of the woman surveyed was 25-45. Also of interest, as the women surveyed got older, for the majority of them, the priority status shifted from their children to their grandchildren.

POP QUIZ

Is it easier to hit a moving or a stationary target planted right in front of you? (And yes, it really is just that simple.) Of course, the answer is—the one sitting right in front of you. Just so ya know mom, most fathers, friends, and siblings are considered *moving targets* by your child. Why? Because they usually won't stand for drama or crap and therefore possess the ability and likelihood of avoiding or moving away from your child should they decide to begin shooting (metaphorically speaking, of course) furthermore, your child *knows this;* they knew it when they were two! But whose love will *always be there* for them no matter what? Who is usually the first one to volunteer to take a bullet for them? Here's a clue—it's the same stationary target that's been sitting in front of them vying for their love, attention and approval their entire life. **THAT'D BE <u>YOU</u> MOM!** Hell, we practically encourage the practice and paint the target on our hearts ourselves, don't we?

Being pleasers, servers, fixers, and rescuers, combined with a mother's inherent love produces an astonishing result—we will actually make ourselves available for *punishment willingly!* We are the ultimate soft target. I recall an honest conversation I once had the privilege of sharing with my adult child about their emotionally neglectful and often-times abrasive or outright verbally abusive behavior toward me. When I asked why it was always aimed at *me,* I was candidly told that it was because they *knew* that I/mom would always love them and be there for them no matter what, that I'd never take my love away, other people, they were not so sure of. I guess it was what you'd call the ultimate backhanded compliment. Many times we mothers make ourselves available to our kids for emotional venting or just plain old bullying; like I said—'*soft target.*'

It is obvious, at least to me, why living for your child/children to the exclusion of just about everything else in your life, and especially yourself and your partner, is absolutely NOT healthy for anyone. Healthy women have many wonderful facets to their personality and their life. And as valuable and irreplaceable as it is, they are also so much more than their role of mother; that is why they must not singularly bond with or solely identify with their role as mother and care giver. What may be harder to see and appreciate is why it is not good for your children either. You may think that being entirely selfless toward your children is highly enlightened, spiritual, Christ-like, Buddha-like, Mother Teresa-Like, or whatever else you may want (or need) to label it, but it isn't. When you send the message to your child or children that they reign supreme, above all others in the family, including and especially you, what do you think you're doing to their highly impressionable ego? What sense of fair-play, humanity and balance, and what level of expectation are you creating for them in their future relationships? Remember, we're talking about the E-generation. They're feeling pretty equal, entitled, and empowered already. So what are you really doing *for them*? What are you promoting or more on-point, what are you doing *to them*? . . . *to their future*? What are you really teaching and accomplishing as a parent if you behave in manner that does not respect you and your marriage/intimate relationship first? What message(s) are you sending? What life lessons are you teaching?

Know this, all the while, every minute of parenthood, you are instructing your child. You are modeling for them how to treat you and how to treat others. Are you teaching them that *they* come first and all other relationships, including the intimate relationship they will one day have, are secondary to their personal needs? Be aware that you are constantly informing them as to the level of respect you deserve, as well as, to what level of expectation they can make demands of you. For parents who are modeling and re-enforcing these negative core values and behaviors, you are putting the very dagger in the hands of your child that may one day pierce your heart. You do this when you teach your child (by example) that you, your identity, your feelings, needs, and welfare do not matter, that everything relative to you, as well as others dear to you, is secondary (if that), and that *they alone come first*. What a terrible thing to teach our children, especially if our desire is that they grow up to be generous, well-balanced, altruistic human beings with a strong sense of themselves and how important it is to honor that in everyone. Remember, kids today are so smart and savvy; they will remember the instruction we give them, as well as the role we embody and model for them. And later, if and when they act out inappropriately, if we are shocked, hurt and don't understand how in the world we could be so self-sacrificing and giving, and yet end up with an adult-child that disrespects us, neglects or abandons us, or abuses us, remember that it's really not a big mystery once we start examining our own contribution to the end-result, no matter how well-intended it may have been at the time.

Back to Lynn's story

Lynn grew up with no father and an emotionally vacant mother who treated her like she was Cinderella but without the prince and the happy ending. Being a lonely child who deeply craved love and approval (the two things her mother withheld from her) Lynn thought that when she had children of her own, all her problems would be solved and her dream of being loved and appreciated would finally come true. She had bought into the fairytale completely and was certain that once she created the family and the love she so desperately wanted, she would never feel unloved, unappreciated, lonely or depressed again. Lynn would be in for a big surprise and major let-down.

There was no doubt that Lynn deeply loved her children, but as many of her friends and eventually her own children would tell you, Lynn was a bottomless pit emotionally. In her pursuit of love and acceptance, Lynn became a super pleaser/giver/rescuer, but because of the black hole and vacuum left in her heart as a result of her childhood, Lynn could never be filled-up or satisfied. Ultimately she became what I call a *bean counter*. If Lynn did **'this'** for you, then you MUST do **'that'** for her; and if *'that'* didn't happen, her ancient feelings of loss and emptiness gushed to the surface and she would attack her friends and family, accusing them of not loving her enough and of not appreciating her kindness. Tragically, nothing was ever quite good enough for Lynn. She always felt that she had drawn the short end of the stick within her relationships and in life in general.

Lynn's need for constant gratitude, acknowledgement, and almost instantaneous pay-back became an emotional addiction that bedeviled her, so much so, that the people in Lynn's life came to dread any act of kindness or generosity on her part. They knew that no matter what they did in return, it would never be enough to ensure that Lynn would not feel hurt, used, taken for granted or taken advantage of. Poor Lynn, she truly had become a bottomless pit. And the saddest irony of all was that although the pit had been there since childhood, the very thing she thought would make it all better (her children) actually made it worse because in Lynn's case, giving and receiving love had become a torture both for her and her children. Love had become a contest where scores were kept and where winners and losers were rewarded or punished as a result of how well they performed. Lynn was giving love in order to get it back, and all in an effort to fill up that dark, hungry pit. But the more she gave, the more she felt unappreciated and the deeper the pit became until finally the void became so great that it could only be described as an all-encompassing vacuum that sucked in everything and everyone around her.

Lynn had six children and pinned her hopes of happiness, love, and contentment on each new baby that came along. Lynn is now in her early sixties and sadly, she still does not get it. Today Lynn is bitter and has no clue why her children and grandchildren keep their distance from her both emotionally and geographically. After all (in her view) all she ever did was *give, give, give,* and all she ever asked for in return was love and appreciation. Lynn is not a bad person at all. She loves her children and grandchildren with all her heart, but, it's a heart that is very damaged and needy, and has never healed. Lynn is in almost constant emotional pain and has even considered taking her own life as a result the sense of grief and loss she experienced when her children withdrew themselves from her life. I thank Lynn for her bravery and honesty, and hope that this book helps her discover a path upon which she will find, forgive, and discover her authentic self and then love and honor that part of herself, as it is her true source of peace, happiness, connection, and meaning in life. Hopefully you too can see how Lynn's inability to honor and heal herself early on in life, resulted in the emotional bottomless pit that destroyed her family. Lynn's life and her continued resentment and intense unhappiness is evidence of why it is not healthy to make your children your sole source of love and validation or your singular reason for living. It is the reason why loving, healing and honoring yourself *must come first* because when you commit to love, heal, and honor yourself, you are also making a commitment to love, heal, and honor your relationship with your children, partner, family and friends. What I have learned (the hard way, by the way) is—

It's never too late to start loving and respecting yourself.

As uncomfortable and unbelievable as it may sound, it really does all start with you. If you do not make 'you' a priority, and by that, I do not mean that you are meant to continue wallowing in your own self-pity and victimhood, nor are you meant to become an unforgiving, thoroughly self-absorbed megalomaniac; no, no, no—just the opposite! You need to pull back those dank, dark heavy drapes and let the sunlight in. You need to first make an honest appraisal of what you've done to contribute to, if not entirely create an environment that allowed things to get out of control with your teen or adult child. Then, remembering to be totally honest with yourself, make a commitment to creating what is best for you and for your children. (Note that I said **best** not *easiest* or *most likeable*.) This is a lifelong project. It took you years to get in the predicament you find yourself in now, and it'll take some time to extract yourself from it. But, again, you must start with *you*. You can start by recognizing and acknowledging if indeed you have been placing your children before everything and everyone else, and if so, break that pattern and change that structure in your life. Begin to *get-to-know yourself* and your partner (if they've hung around through all this drama). Let your adult child know that, howbeit late in life, you are setting new and healthy boundaries and behavioral expectations that will ultimately serve you both in life and in your relationship, and will remain lovingly and consistently in place.

What if your adult child walks away from you?

When it comes to your E-generation children (tween, teen or adult) this metamorphosis is likely going to go over like the proverbial lead balloon. These children have run this country you're living in as an indentured servant for a long time and now you want it back? Sister, that's quite a civil uprising you're inciting. And as the world learned in 2011, some dictators quickly get the message, and out of love for their country and its people, graciously step down, and then there are those *other dictators.* They're the ones who will fight to the bitter end in order to maintain their power; some will even massacre the very people they say they love and are there to serve and protect. Sound familiar? If so, as both a historical reference and cautionary tale: most parents I have spoken with are living in Libya not Egypt. So if bombs are suddenly dropped on you when you announce that you want your country back, remember that sometimes, doing the right thing, the thing that's best for everyone concerned, also means pissing some people off. So if you need to, take cover and take heart; and know that you're not alone, reinforcements are on the way. It is also important to know that once your children become adults, and once you've set some boundaries, if they elect *not* to respect them, or if they choose to behave badly, it is no longer your duty to digress into the role of pleaser/fixer, or victim for that matter. Remember, that's what created the problem in the first place. You must remain strong, and perhaps for the first time in your life, choose to respect yourself and your decision(s) and stand by them. And by doing so, respect your adult child as well. Choose to place yourself and your partner first. Choose to put what is right and authentically loving for both you and your children first.

They say there are no guarantees in life, however one thing is certain (and you know it already)—doing what you've been doing, doesn't work. So try something else! Try something new! Remember, people do not respect someone who does not respect themselves, period. So maybe it's time for you to step up and be the parent you were meant to be, and more importantly, be the person you owe it to yourself to be. Be the partner you are meant to be. Focus on those areas of your new life. When there's been time for reflection and growth, and when your child *(hopefully)* comes to realize they can no longer manipulate or control you via your neediness and willingness to please and serve, when they realize that mom deserves and now requires the same love and respect she has always given them, perhaps then, there will be a healthy transformation in your relationship with your adult child. I would love to say that your adult child will return to you and spend the rest of their life giving you the respect and love you so richly deserve and that in turn, you will give them space and healthy love they need and so richly deserve. But people are unpredictable, and that means that in spite of your best efforts and your amazing growth and autonomy, your wayward child may not return to you on the timetable you'd prefer, or, they may not return at all. The potential does exist for them to walk out of your life completely, that's the hard but simple truth. If that happens, you need to take heart and know that all things work together for the good, and then turn it over to your higher power. As long as your children know that you love them and are there for them when they can respect you and the reasonable and healthy boundaries you have put in place, then you have done the loving/right thing and the ball is now in their court, and hard as it will be at times, there you must leave it.

You will have pain but know that this is a time for personal and spiritual growth, for growing and expanding as a human being and spiritually, not only for you, but for your child too. They say that which does not destroy you makes you stronger. I would add that you must see a higher purpose in the events you experience. You can interpret events as an *ending* or as a *beginning*; as a door opening or closing for you, as either a catastrophe or a catalyst for positive change and growth. So rather than seeing the suspension or a anguished ending of a relationship, focus on what is *beginning* for you and your family as a result of your spirit-based choices and current circumstances. Know that it is a healing time and accept and embrace it in that spirit. For me, it was time to finally focus on my personal goals, to learn more about what makes *me* tick and what makes Kay happy. Also, rather than seeing my child *going away from me* as or viewing our experience as an ending or door slamming shut, I choose to see it as a door opening, as a new beginning. As entry into a place where we will both grow and one day come together in a place of mutual love and respect. I accepted my current situation and transformed it from a *'sad state of affairs'* into *an amazing gift*. Granted, it was a hard gift to embrace at first, but with time, I did, and as it turns out, it was one of life's richest gifts, both for me and I have no doubt for my child and their ultimate growth too.

The Gift

I was a consummate Super-pleaser/fixer/servant/rescuer extraordinaire who never developed my own interests or a life and identity independent of my children. The gift my child gave me when they took their love away and distanced themselves from me was the gift of *time*, time to let them grow, time to expand as a person (for both them and me), time for me to learn that my marriage came first, time to get to know my husband, and again (and incredibly) to get to know and learn to love and honor myself for the very first time in my life. It's all about perspective; reality is what you make it. Whatever meaning you attach to an event, situation, condition or relationship becomes your truth, your reality, and live *that reality* you will, no matter how healthy or unhealthy it may be. I became dedicated to transforming my reality for the better, and as I grew, I became equally determined to become a force for good, to use my experiences to enrich and empower other mothers who found themselves feeling empty, isolated, and less-than-great about the status of their relationship with their teen or adult child. So please, embrace this experience and trust in the process. This could be a time for grieving and loss or a time of massive growth and reconnection to yourself, your partner and your God. Don't get me wrong, there's a place for the stages of grief and loss, but eventually they must give way to growth and a higher purpose, otherwise they're for naught. That is why I encourage you to embrace your life situation as a chance for you to re-prioritize your life.

Turning a catastrophe into a catalyst for growth and ultimate good

Our suffering can smack us down to the ground and empty out our soul or it can deepen our connection to God/our higher power and our higher purpose. It can strengthen our character and create in us (and in you) a determination to change our situation, to transform our life, and to touch the lives of others. That is the powerful lesson we can take from all this. When I think of the gifts and immeasurable growth that are available to you as a result of your being at this painful place on your path, I pray you choose the gifts. And while you are embracing that, know too, that even with your commitment to see the good, to create an opening, to grow and contribute, you will of course experience sorrow and pain, it comes with owning a mother's heart. It's what you do with the pain that matters. For me, when that pain came, and when I beat myself up for not being stronger, for not leaving my children's father sooner or for the abuse we endured and for my crippling victimhood, I remembered the words of my dear friend Marianne: *"this is my first life too."* I comforted and assured myself with those words. I made peace with *me* first, then spoke my truth to my children, offered them love, set healthy boundaries, offered reconciliation and counseling (together or separately) if they wanted it. I also exorcised the ghosts of my own past and developed a mantra I repeated to myself whenever self pity, loneliness, bitterness, or grief threatened to infest my thoughts and take over my emotions.

> *Under their dysfunction, their damaged-ness & pain*
> *as well as their own stories, beliefs & filters*
> *I know my children deeply love me.*

If my child behaved badly or hurt me deeply, I would repeat that mantra until it was integrated into my subconscious and had become a safe haven for my emotions. I would pray, send out love to my child, and then lovingly surrender my circumstances and my child to spirit and to their highest good, knowing that winter lasts but a season and darkness but a night and joy comes in the morning. I learned to trust fully that all things work together for our ultimate spiritual growth and good.

If you are presently estranged from your adult child, you too, can develop a routine or ritual that works best for you. But do please know that life is a process, and so is this pain you're experiencing, it is part of a growth process for you emotionally, socially, and spiritually. Likewise, it is part of your child's life journey and education as well. Take heart, trust in that, and know that the pain will not last forever; that darkness always gives way to the light. You are a beautiful, strong, and capable woman, and you've made it this far in life, so let's keep going!

CHAPTER 16

Lying & Other Issues
that Negatively Impact Parenting

A total commitment to rigorous, consistent HONESTY is a must

If a relationship does not have total honesty as the foundation upon which it is built, it has nothing. The commitment to, and the exercise of honesty in your life creates from itself an environment of integrity, and integrity is the stuff that *inner strength* and *character* are made of. Take a moment to think about all the other admirable and enduring qualities of a solid relationship and you will see that they all arise from honesty and integrity. When a person *knows* they can rely 100% on the honesty of their partner in all things, that builds respect and trust, and in turn respect and trust breed loyalty. That powerful combination then gives birth to an atmosphere of comfort and ease within the relationship. Absent a commitment to honesty, there can be no ease, no comfort, no respect, and certainly no trust or loyalty. Hence the saying: *"I trust him about as far as I can throw him!"*—what does that statement really mean? It means that person has been identified as a liar and thus untrustworthy, thereby forfeiting any and all trust the speaker had in them.

Do not allow lying to go un-checked and unaddressed

Whether it's your partner, child, sibling or friend, if they lie to you about insignificant things, they'll lie about the significant things too. Whoever the subject of your concern may be, pay close attention to their communications. If a person makes a practice of lying about the little things (about stuff they don't need to lie about) it's not a far stretch to assume that they're lying to you about the big stuff too. It is also true that when someone lies to you regularly and haphazardly (lying about anything and everything) they are usually also lying about other people, events or circumstances in their life as well. Don't be naïve, if your loved one is not being honest with others or is scandalously disingenuous or duplicitous in other relationships, they're more than likely also lying to and about you as well. It's just a sad but simple truth about the way lying works and demonstrates itself as a habit in a person's life who has allowed the practice to flourish. The problem inside families is that once lying goes unchecked either because a parent is too lazy to investigate or too apathetic to address it, that marks the beginning of a hailstorm of lies and drama to follow. Because lying is such an insidious disease, parents and partners should hold it in the same esteem as a cancer or the plague because that's how deadly it can be in person's life and the health of their relationships if allowed to proliferate. If stealing, drug abuse, alcoholism, or physical abuse was occurring with regularity, you would take action and execute an intervention, would you not? Then please, set a good example yourself by practicing loving, yet vigorous/rigorous honesty in your life, and from there, encourage its growth and allow it to spread and bloom within your family and relationships, because without it, integrity and true quality of relating/relationships does not exist, only facades that look like relationships and the superficiality that glosses itself over them instead of a healthy, authentic connection and bond to the people in your life.

I can change them!

A lesson that took many years and entailed multiple frustrating let-downs before it was finally learned was that—we cannot change another person. That truth is plain and simple, yet profoundly true and essential to learn. You may have tried to change your spouse, your children, or other family members. You may have even tried to change your friends and have no doubt discovered that it doesn't work. We as women often learn the hard way that we cannot force enlightenment, growth, or change on another human being. We know the futility of this effort because most of us have been trying to change our partners for years! Among adults, genuine growth and change just doesn't take place that way. In spite of that fact, can we practice loving, yet rigorous honesty and set a positive example? Of course. Can we offer assistance should a person be inclined to seek guidance? Again, of course we can. What we absolutely cannot and should not do is *force* our will, ideologies, or our love down another person's throat, not unless we're also prepared to have it spit back in our face when they choke on it.

There's an old Buddhist saying—*when the student is ready, the teacher will appear.* I've come to rely upon truths like this to see me through the confusing, challenging or hurtful times that come with being human and especially accompany parenthood. Once your children are adults, they own their own lives and destiny; therefore, it is no longer our privilege, job, or right to impose our will on them, even if our information, approach, and intentions are one hundred percent right and pure. Having said that, there are a few exceptions, such as *family intervention* for a member who is abusing drugs or alcohol, but even then, it is ultimately the choice of the family member confronted with the truth *(whatever that truth may be)* as to whether or not they'll embrace the intervention and make the necessary changes. So any illusion we have of power or the ability to force change and growth on our children, or anyone else for that matter, is just that—an illusion.

All authentic and lasting growth must have its inception inside the heart of the person who desires it and is dedicated to personal growth and transformation. It's not enough that *you* desire it. It's a tough pill to swallow but it's the truth. But again, that's not to say that there are not things you can do in your life that will present a strong and positive role model for your adult child. The healing you want for your heart will not come from your child being struck by a magic bullet and then suddenly seeing things your way or by them behaving in a manner that superficially pleases you or makes you feel loved for the moment but is not authentic. That type of placation is a kind of superficial enrichment that lasts only a short-while because it's coming to you from the outside in rather than radiating from the inside out. Relations that fall into that category are like the weather, they can change in an instant. The only person you have the power to change is the one holding this book, that's why the wiser path is to begin the healing process by creating a foundational love and respect for yourself because that's where all transformational change begins—with you.

How low self esteem can play a role in abusive relationships with adult children

You didn't just wake up one morning and find that your formerly adoring and respectful child is now a tyrant who verbally abuses, uses, and/or neglects you. I believe that some character weaknesses and behaviors are inherent in all human beings but that many of our bad habits are learned. Somehow, somewhere along the line, your child was taught that it's okay to treat you in a disrespectful or neglectful way, in fact, they may have actually been intentionally or inadvertently rewarded for doing it. Not only that, they may have also grown to feel perfectly free to make selfish or unreasonable demands of you and to expect immediate gratification. When this dynamic exists and persists it's because there was/is a positive pay off for them whenever they exhibit disturbing or demanding behavior. That's why we all do *'whatever it is we do'* on a regular basis—because we get some kind of payoff from it. When a three year old throws a colossal tantrum in a store with the result being that they *earn* the toy or candy they were screaming for, you are actively teaching them that demanding, tyrannical behavior works and will ultimately get them what they want in life. That's why I use the word *'earn'* to describe the child's intentions and actions; have no doubt, there is an exchange taking place. That three year old is focused and working hard for what it is they want and be sure of one thing, they'll invest a tremendous amount of positive or negative energy either way and whatever it takes in order to achieve their goal. They're *earning it* and you're providing the payoff. Can you see how allowing bad behavior to result in a positive payoff sets the stage for an unhealthy indoctrination for both you and your child?

The lower a parent's self esteem and sense of strength and purpose in raising their child, the more prone they are to turning all the power over to the child. When did you first violate a boundary or give into an unacceptable behavior or worse yet, reward it? Why? Was it due to low self esteem, neediness, laziness, or some other dynamic that was at play? What did you think would grow from that small act, oversight, or incident? Did you think about it at all? My guess is, it was not an isolated incident and that the behavior escalated over the years until your son or daughter grew into an extremely well trained Master in the art of manipulation. The saddest casualty of this kind of authority shift in parent child relations is *respect*. When someone cannot respect themselves and does not require it from others, including their own children, they become unworthy of respect, particularly from the point of view of those taking advantage of them. There is no *up-side* to weakness in parenting. As we established earlier, people admire and respect strength, particularly inner strength and character. What does that say about us mothers, when we (out of what we call 'love') allow our children to be harsh task masters who make demands or manipulate us in order to get what they want? *That is not love!* It is not love and respect for you and it certainly is not an act of love and respect for your child when you allow it. Laziness, fear, low self esteem, neediness or a combination of those dynamics play key roles in the development of this destructive power shift between parent and child.

The emotionally lazy parent

You know who I'm talking about. We've all seen them at the park before. They're the parent who squats on a park bench and refuses to get up and play with their child. They don't toss the ball; they don't go to school plays, ballet recitals, sporting events, or school drives, and they're always too busy to read a book to their children or watch a Disney movie with them. When their toddler throws a tantrum, they don't address the behavior one way or the other because they're just too lazy or embarrassed to do the work of being a responsible parent. We've all had to sit next to them or behind them on a plane or in a movie theater. They're the parent that does not take their screaming child for a stroll down the aisle to soothe them or remove them from the theater out of care and consideration, first for their child, and then out of consideration for their fellow passengers or movie goers. That kind of commitment to parenting is just not in their repertoire, and for that, everyone around them suffers. Parents who are *on the job* are not only accustomed to practicing honesty and saying *"no"* when needed (and meaning it) but also to enduring the emotional and civil revolt that often follows. Parents who are on the ball do not just 'endure,' they endeavor to teach their child and transform the negative behavior and experience into a valuable life lesson for them. What a difference attitude and approach can make. For the lazy, uninvolved parent, it's easier to ignore bad behavior or give-in, in order to appease their child and quiet their protests. In order to curtail an unpleasant encounter/situation with their child, these parents will either tune out the bad behavior altogether or take the path of least resistance by giving in to the unacceptable behavior. Unlike the parent who gives in as a result of low self esteem and a dire need to please and be accepted, lazy parents are simply not invested in their child's growth and the development of their character.

Gender differences & low self esteem

While performing research and meeting dozens of parents, I've come across data that is both fascinating and confusing. By and large, men/fathers are more likely to be uninvolved or take the path of least resistance when it comes to child rearing when the children are young. Although they can be very opinionated and insistent in some situations, most often, fathers were either indifferent or powerless marshmallows when it came to matters concerning parenting during the early years, particularly when it came to their daughters. Mothers on the other hand, gave-in less often during the early years. They were generally tougher than dad when the kids were younger. However, mom's role relative to her children changes dramatically as the years go by. An astonishing trend has anecdotally emerged from my research. Fathers remained aloof relative to the nitty-gritty details of parenting; and where mothers used to be the gatekeeper and hands-on parent, guardian, disciplinarian, and keeper of the peace, as the years went on and her sense of power and control waned, mom grew positionally weaker and was less regarded by her children. This emotional transition seemed to occur in direct proportion to mom's increasing loss of identity and subsequent need for her children's unconditional love and validation. Most ironic and interesting, at the end of the day, as children grow older and move into adulthood, and in spite of the disparity in hands-on parenting between mom and dad, fathers were more likely to be the recipient of what I call *global respect* from their children.

The respect ratio offers an odd juxtaposition, especially when one considers that mothers are known to be exceptionally tender-hearted and loyal to a fault, and yet, at the same time, in our heart of hearts we can also be pretty tough when we have to, *but* . . . only it seems, during the younger, impressionable years. We endure nine months of pregnancy and child birth; we nurse, pamper, care for and raise our children (often alone) and we bear the scars (emotional and physical) of that passage for the rest of our lives. We are, by no means weaklings. So what is it that propels us toward subservient behaviors and submissiveness relative to our children as they grow older? The answer lies in the depth of our hearts and the unconditional love we have for our children. I believe those qualities, when not administered properly help to set the stage for problems later in life. It's sad to consider that our need to give and receive love may later be employed by our children to manipulate or hurt us. Based on history, facts, and the real life experiences of dozens of mothers, I believe there are two specific things that occur that place a mother at higher risk for developing a unhealthy relationship with their children later in life.

1. Low self esteem or some other emotional factor creates an extreme need for some mothers to make their children their primary or singular source of identity and reason for living, often to the exclusion of everything else. These mothers cultivate a reality for themselves wherein their primary or singular source of genuine love, meaning, and self worth comes solely from their child and nothing but a satisfactory connection to their child and gratification of those needs will fill them up. (*Most men do not do this.*)

2. As the result of this deeply held belief system and extreme codependency, unless mom is constantly being filled up with love, self worth, and a sense of meaning by her child, she begins to feel groundless and empty; that is a terrifying place to be for a mother who has dedicated her entire life to her role as mother.

When this paradigm shift occurs, life becomes a desperate race not to lose control or lose the love they've so deeply and desperately invested themselves in. If that connection and satisfaction is lost, these mothers feel unloved, worthless, and empty. That's when any self-respect, as well as any respect the child had, is sacrificed at the altar of mom's emotional needs. Consequently, mom becomes a vacuum, a bottomless pit that can never be filled. This potentially sets the stage for condescension, manipulation, verbal abuse, neglect, and ultimately estrangement to occur as relations continue to deteriorate.

It's nearly impossible for an adult child to respect a person who has no sense of themselves as an individual and no self respect. When the once strong, reliable role model, rule maker/keeper, and parent, becomes a needy Super-pleaser, respect is lost. And although motivated by love, there is also something else that's powering this locomotive, and that is raw, naked, desperate *need*. Mom needs to feel that love flowing to her, filling her up and making her feel important, cared for, needed, and valuable, and if that all-consuming need entails taking some *'guff'* from her kid or settling for any emotional crumbs that may drop from the table, most moms will obediently accept and adjust to their new role (in the back seat or trunk). They do it because *being a mom* and feeling connected to, and an integral a part of their child's life is all these mothers have ever known and is all they ever wanted. Many of them desperately need is to feel loved, needed, accepted, and validated by their children no matter the personal cost. Sadly, the more emotionally needy we become, the more available we make ourselves for manipulation, for being taken for granted, and the more available we become for being taken advantage of. Ironically, the more you try to please, fix, serve, and rescue, the more distain your child may ultimately feel and exhibit toward you as a result of your weakness and misguided efforts. It is not that they don't love you; it's the weakness of your character they are responding negatively to. It becomes a vicious cycle where balance and genuine success as a parent will never be experienced unless the pattern is broken. As an acclaimed authority on raising children once said *"I don't know the key to success, but the key to failure is trying to please everyone."*

Remember the difference between the two types of mothers we talked about earlier: One kept her own identity, interests, and life outside her children. She still loved her children, but in a way that was healthy for both herself and her children. And when it came time to say *NO* and really mean it, she was able to do that, and ultimately, that is what earned her the healthy love and respect she now enjoys with her children. Whereas our second mother, who made the two fatal mistakes referenced in this chapter set up the foundation of parenthood on very shaky, unpredictable ground. Your children should not be your primary or solitary source of love, identity, self esteem, or meaning in life, and just as, if not more important to understand and accept-you too, should not be (or expect to be) their primary or solitary source of love, identity, self esteem, or meaning in life.

Children are a part of the wonderful mosaic that is your life but must never become the single conduit through which you experience your life, love, joy or meaning. To set your life up in that way is to create a bottomless pit existence for yourself and your children.

Are you a bottomless pit?

The most profound lessons I learned through my experiences were:

First—realizing that I fell into the category of mothers who had made the two critical parenting errors.

Second—When you set up another person to be your primary reason for living and your sole source of love, joy, validation etc., you not only do yourself, but your children an incredible disservice. You, in effect, set the clock on a ticking time bomb that will one day explode. Beyond that, if you're really honest with yourself, if this is how you set up your life and your relationship with your child, then eventually, even *your love* becomes a tool and sometimes a weapon in the internal battle you're waging to get your needs met. To make matters worse, because the only love that counted for you was the love of your children, you either consciously or subconsciously disqualified other people and sources of love available to you over the years. This made it even more crucial that you get the love you need from what you've designated as the primary or singular source—your child.

When your love becomes tainted by your own unhealthy personal needs, it is then at risk of being used as a pawn, tool, or weapon. Add to that the fact that you more than likely helped create a very self-indulgent E-generation adult child, you now have all the elements necessary to manifest a perfect storm. You have become an empty vacuum that *must be filled* by your child exclusively because if you are not, life (as you've designed it) has little or no meaning. Getting the love you need, as you define it (from your child) becomes a matter of emotional life and death, and sometimes even physical life or death, as we saw so tragically in Jennifer's story. When caught up in your neediness and woundedness, you become a bottomless pit; an emotional black hole where love must flow to you and can only come from one primary or solitary source, otherwise you are left unfulfilled and miserable. That, my friend, is a pit that will never be filled; it's also an agonizingly painful and unfulfilling place to spend your life. Once you get to this point, regardless of what you did right or wrong with your child in the past or whether your adult child is a loving, respectful, luminescent, evolved soul or a not-so-beaming example of a demanding, spoiled rotten E-generation brat does not matter, because regardless of your adult child's personality, emotional/social status, it remains a fact that no one (good, bad, or indifferent) can sustain a relationship with a person for whom they have become their singular reason for living. No one can fill up a bottomless pit, nor is it their responsibility to.

One path to balance and health for mothers who find themselves defined above is to consider taking on the following challenges.

1. *You* must begin to fill yourself up and no longer make that someone else's responsibility.
2. You must redefine your role of mother.
3. You must redefine and embrace what it means to be a strong, capable independent woman.
4. You must redefine what it means to be loved.
5. Most importantly, you must create other avenues through which you can give and receive the love and validation we all need, crave, and deserve in life.

CHAPTER 17

Learning to Accept that as a Parent, You did the Best You Could with the Life Experiences, Education, Tools & Resources You Had

The first step—An honest assessment

Okay, it's time to come clean. Did you get up every single morning of your life, and while preparing for your day or as you sat at the table or in your car drinking your morning coffee, did you focus all your attention on how you could make your child's life a living hell that day? Did you willfully conspire to destroy their sense of safety or self esteem? Did you let your mind run wild with all the names you could call them or ways you could destroy their trust in, and respect for you?

Thank God, the answer to those questions has consistently been an indignant and resounding *"No, of course not!"* Good mothers are offended by the mere suggestion that they could even be capable of such malice. The truth is, most mothers did just the opposite, we sought to make our children's lives and their childhood *better* than our own had been. We kept our kids clean, fed, safe, and gave them everything we possibly could. We would readily give our lives for our children. And woe unto the unknowing soul that dared to put our children in any kind of real or perceived jeopardy because that's when the momma bear in us rears her head and exposes her claws. We love our children and want only the best for them each and every day of their childhood and for the rest of their lives. My prayer for my children is the same today as it was the day they were born—that they always be healthy, happy, and safe from harm.

When to hold yourself responsible and when not to

If you intentionally did things that resulted in a loss of trust and respect, then you need to own that and work to make amends and rebuild the love, trust, and respect you lost. But, let me say this loud and clear—when a mother has raised her child or children in an environment of love, commitment, and trust, and with the best of paternal intentions, and does it passionately and with the only *education*, tools, and resources available to her (which may be scant) then that mother should hold her head high and take great pride and comfort in the knowledge that she did her absolute best. That goes for you dads too. *'Education'* does not refer to ones higher education or academic accomplishments. The education I am referring to is the one you got when you were a child. Your early childhood experiences with your own parents constitutes your parental training *(i.e., 'education')* and manifests as your own **How to Parent Manual** that you consciously or subconsciously draw from later in life. What's so crazy about this is that many times our ideas of parenting aren't even our own, they have been passed down to us by our parents, and to them, by their parents. Some of these inherited parenting tenets and practices are antiquated, some are sage advice, and a lot of it is inappropriate or downright wrong. So if you're a mom who wasn't raised by emotionally healthy and emotionally present and generous parents herself and didn't have a story-book childhood yourself but genuinely did the best you could and tried to avoid the pit-falls of your parents, then it's time to let go of the guilt you may be feeling and may have been carrying in your heart for years. Guilt is an incapacitatingly heavy burden to bear and does not serve you or your child's ultimate good, so quit lugging it around.

There are no perfect human beings and therefore no perfect parents out there, period, end of story. Everyone does the best they can with the life experiences and tools they possess. Therefore, if your love has been true and consistent and your efforts well-intended and noble, then let go of the guilt. Quit blaming yourself for life experiences outside of your control or for the poor choices your adult child is making or has made in their life. Quit blaming yourself for their lack of initiative, failure(s), poor quality of relationships, bad choices, and life circumstances, as well as their upsets and anger at you. In short, it's time to quit your job as designated soft target, victim, and resident scapegoat.

Understanding your adult child's behavior and de-personalizing it

E-generation children grew up experiencing instant gratification, empowerment and entitlement as a kind of birthright while at the same time suffering through a virtual collapse of the traditional family. Often times, this resulted in E-kids raising themselves or growing up in a day-care or after-school care centers. Considering the mixture of all these social/emotional dynamics, it's not hard to see how a rather large chip could develop on the shoulder of an E-generation child when their needs and expectations were not met. And by *met*, I mean manifested as *they* deem they should be. The E-generation learned to determine their own likes, dislikes, as well as their own personal/social values and needs, and how they should be met. They learned this via institutional instruction *(as to their rights, etc.)* MTV and/or cable television, outspoken/ graphic or controversial music lyrics, television, movies, violent or (what I call—) 'conscious numbing' video games, the internet and their peers, as well as the commercial media's hardcore marketing push to sell a very materialistic, ego-based lifestyle to them. The E-generation strove to define itself via what brand they wore, what they listened to, watched, read, and what they consumed, and none said it better than the 'material girl' herself. No wonder that it can be an uphill battle when a parent tries to reason with them or draws a line in the sand regarding inappropriate behavior.

Maybe you were working or going to school, or like me, worked two day-jobs while also going to college at night. As a single mom with no extended family or resources to help me raise my children, my kids, like many others, were missing a full-time mom. That leaves a lot of time for kids to make up their own rules and establish their own expectations in life. It also lends itself to the development of *resentment*; after all, kids require love, attention, structure, and guidance. Structure is so important to children and if there is a lack of it and an absence of established parental hierarchy, trouble is not far off. The truth about the need for structure and stability is not mentioned so as to make an already exhausted, hard-working parent feel worse, it's simply a fact of life and of parenting and therefore must be shared. I'm sure that like me, many parents simply had no choice in the matter; they had to work two, sometimes three jobs to keep a roof over their child's head. Out of a deep desire to provide a better life for themselves and their children, many parents/mothers like me made the difficult choice of working and attending school at the same time. This is an emotionally charged, challenging, and thoroughly exhausting position to be placed in, and not just physically and academically, but most importantly, relative to spending cherished time with one's children, especially when we know how fast the precious years of childhood pass. If you are currently in, or have been in this position in the past, then you know how precious those years are and may be feeling incredibly guilty and deprived as a result of not having more time with your children. If you did what I later did, you overcompensated by becoming a super pleaser/server/fixer/rescuer and/or by deciding to *go easy* on mischievous, disrespectful, and/or challenging behavior. I called it *practicing unconditional love* and I did it by allowing my children to feel and be equal to me, and to be freely and totally self-expressed, even critical and sometimes down-right rude toward me without consequence. I also avoided negative confrontations at all costs. As to why I did this, the answer came to me easily and seemed logical. In addition to my own 'original abandonment' issues and divorce-guilt, I wanted our time together to be a positive/happy experience for my children. I certainly did not want my limited time with my children to be spent with them angry at me for being a parent.

Adding to my laundry list of reasons for abdicating the throne—I was raised under the unhealthy but strictly enforced belief that children were to be seen and not heard and I hated it! I decided I would never do that to my kids, only in my case, I took it to the next level which was equally unhealthy. When they would break a rule or behave disrespectfully, and considering my lack of quality time with them, and not wanting conflict, I caved-in. Rather than seeing it as a dangerous lack of parenting or being a wimp on my part, I labeled my behavior *unconditional love*. I wanted to be their *'friend,'* another big mistake. If you mix super pleaser/server qualities with an attempt to earn your child's friendship via permissive behavior that you erroneously label *unconditional love* or being a *cool parent*, what you're really doing is crying out for love and acceptance. A *friend* or a *cool parent* is not what your child needs; they need a parent, they need structure, they need to know that there are laws that govern this country we call family and that they're there because you love them. If like me, you made this mistake, be honest with yourself and begin to acknowledge and appreciate all that you have created and have allowed to proliferate. Begin to see that by doing so, you may have inadvertently created the very environment that gave birth to the teen or adult child you are now used, abused, berated, ignored and/or hurt by. Being totally honest and then identifying the source of a problem or condition is the first step in coming to terms with it. Once that is done, you can learn and grow from your life and parenting experiences. As you continue on your path of self awareness, you will grow and move past the obstacles that stand in the way of your sense of well-being, inner happiness, and peace, both as a parent, and more importantly as the wonderful, independent, self-aware woman you can grow into being.

Forgiving yourself and remembering—this is your first life too

It's a pretty simple philosophy. Just remember and remind yourself that this really is your first lifetime too. We were not born into perfection, nor were any of us given a magical key that would unlock all the wisdom and right choices to make as a human being or as a parent. That is why acknowledging and accepting that you did the best job you could given the experiences, obstacles, challenges, and events of your own childhood and adult life, as well as the available tools and resources (or lack thereof) available to you at the time, is both a good and essential context in which to process the reality that life and circumstances with your adult child are not ideal right now.

Your life experiences, education, tools, and resources

Integral to forgiving yourself is an understanding that you, like most mothers reading this book, were raised in a very different time and with drastically different standards. If your inherent beauty and value was not recognized and celebrated, if your self esteem was not bolstered, if you were punished or ridiculed rather than complimented, praised, and encouraged, if you were beaten down instead of bathed in love, acceptance, and tenderness, then sadly, it is not likely that you will inherently possess a positive parental frame of reference and life/parenting education, and it's *not* your fault. On the bright side, what that does leave you with is a frame of reference from which you do not wish to raise your children; a laundry list of what you *don't want* for your child, and what you *don't want* is what *you* experienced as a child. Many parents who raised children from this place are often times flying blind because they simply are not aware of or personally acquainted with what it's like to experience a loving, nurturing childhood first-hand, and those, my friends, are some of the best tools a parent can possess.

Cooking without a recipe

To raise a child without an established/healthy frame of reference is like attempting to make a sumptuous gourmet dinner without having the ingredients necessary for preparing such a flawless delight. And as if that wasn't challenging enough, for many of us, not only do we *not* have the prime ingredients in our repertoire, we don't have the recipe, in fact, we don't even own a cookbook! When faced with that predicament and challenge, yet still deeply desiring to create the masterpiece, our passion leads us as we follow our heart and diligently do the best job we can with resources available to us. And if I may say so, most of us took on the challenge, worked hard and passionately, envisioned the dream, kept the faith. We labored in love to prepare the very best feast we knew how to make, and for that effort, we should be very proud. Acknowledge and celebrate the fact that you took on and lovingly did the challenge and responsibility of parenting. You owned your job mom, and for that you can hold your head high. You worked diligently to make the masterpiece and you gave it your all. Please remember and honor yourself for that. You did the absolute very best you could with the ingredients you had available to you, and because of that valiant effort and the tenacity of your love and efforts, you were/are a good mother. So please, when your heart is heavy with guilt, forgive yourself for your deficiencies. As we said at the start of this chapter, you didn't get up every morning and plot to ruin your child's life and future. You took on the world's hardest job, and may have done it alone, but you did it to the absolute best of your abilities, and whether good, bad, or indifferent, you did it with the only education, tools, and resources you had available to you, and for that, I honor and salute you.

Forgiving your teen or adult child

Now that you've hopefully cut yourself some slack, it's time to consider your child. You remember them, that person you gave birth to; that beloved and adorable child who was a source of supreme pleasure and pride when they were little, and now, may at times be a source of extreme pain and heartache for you? Depending on how much your relationship has deteriorated, it wouldn't be surprising if they've lost the title of beloved and are occasionally called *other names* now and then. Relax, and remember—it's not only okay, it's *healthy* to have a good laugh and a sense of humor and optimism about all this; it can even be therapeutic.

Who better to start off a chat about forgiveness with then Jesus Christ, who after suffering terrible abuses and just moments from death, said of his abusers *"Father forgive them, for they know not what they do."* Not only are those magnanimous and powerful words both thought and growth provoking, they are also a wonderful analogy and point of reference for beleaguered parents, especially mothers.

Most E-generation teens and young adult children are self-absorbed and wrapped up in *their own lives, their friends,* and *their story,* so much so that they can hardly be expected (at least in their view) to consider such mundane and unnecessary things like maturity, introspection and self growth, let alone objectively consider the feelings of others. On top of that, in order to keep their stories safely intact, they must have someone at the ready to blame and punish. In the lives of tweens, teens, and many young adults, there is inevitably a good guy and bad guy, a victor and a villain, a shooter and a target; a hero and scapegoat. Guess who the scapegoat is? That's right, most of the time it's you, the walking talking soft target known as *mom*. Quickest, best advice available-stop volunteering to be a soft target, scapegoat, or stand-in for the family dog that gets kicked whenever your teen or adult child is upset. That's a good first step because aside from changing your focus and energies, setting proper boundaries will help pave the way to self growth, genuine forgiveness, and authentic healing because you won't feel or be preoccupied with your sense of resentment or victimhood all the time. You need to also recognize that if you've helped to set up the dysfunctional/manipulative or abusive relationship, then you also need to take some responsibility for it. After all, you helped shape and mold the spoiled E-generation scoundrel who now, rather than bringing you love and joy, has become an emotional or financial pestilence in your life.

Now it's *your turn* to suck it up and acknowledge whether or not this rings true for you or not mom. Also know that under our humorous labeling and your child's dysfunction and stories, your child does love you, to what depth or degree varies, as does the quality and measure of that love's healthiness, but do be sure, there is history and love there. Knowing and appreciating this, you must find the willingness to forgive yourself and your wayward child because it is essential to your physical and emotional survival, as well as your future growth and happiness.

A Wonderful Buddhist adage

> *If you throw hot coals at your enemy*
> *You may or may not hit & injure them*
> *But you are certain to burn yourself*

For our purpose, the hot coals represent un-forgiveness. The mere act of keeping them, of stoking the fire to keep them hot, and then taking them into your own hand to hurl at others will burn you to the depth of your soul, and for what? The target of your un-forgiveness may or may not be hit or injured by the hot coal you throw at them but you will surely be burnt as a result of your actions. You only hurt and scar yourself when you make un-forgiveness your companion and guide in life. To forgive others, especially the ones that have hurt us the most, is to set yourself free. However, forgiving others does not mean that you allow abusive behavior to continue. You can and must set boundaries and lovingly insist on their enforcement while continuing to love with all your heart. The difference is, you are now loving and respecting yourself too, maybe for the first time in your life.

During the course of this journey with yourself and your child, you may have to forgive them and love them from a distance should they not respond positively to your personal insights, growth, and establishment of healthy boundaries. If that happens, you must take care of yourself and choose to see the experience as a new beginning in your life rather than an ending. Your love is always available to them and they must know that, but, they must also know, accept, and respect that you are no longer available for target practice, venting, abuse, disrespect, manipulation, or unnecessary drama.

Creating a place of healing for you and your children

Many parents, when taking that first gigantic step toward healthy change in an unhealthy or abusive relationship with their child, will call them and *get clear* with them on the phone or see them in person, others will write a long heart-felt letter. Other parents feel compelled to take drastic action when it comes to correcting a troubled or abusive relationship with their child. I have heard stories of parents who have taken aggressive action, such as: telling their adult child that they must move out of their house, cutting off financial support, refusing to bail them out, taking the car they *(the parent)* paid for away. Some parents have elected to quit their job as nursemaid, butler, babysitter, maid, cook, secretary, accountant, or chauffeur. Paramount in your progress is taking the bull's-eye off your heart. Remember—you're no longer a soft target.

How a parent decides to extract themselves from a disrespectful, dangerous, or hurtful situation or environment is as individual as the dynamics and personal needs of all the parties involved. Having said that, do be sure that taking a loving stand is the first step toward creating boundaries, balance, respect, healing and ultimately reconciliation. You must stop the negative or abusive cycle, set reasonable/healthy boundaries, and maintain them. Once your adult child comes to realize that you are not simply threatening or whining, and that you're not throwing a tantrum or acting out (which you may have done in the past), they will begin to see you shining in the new light of self respect and full awareness. While that transformation is making itself real in your life and in your child's mind, you need to become your own source of healing and growth. Contrary to your former way of being, both with your child and others in your life, you must now put yourself and your authentic needs first.

★ By authentic, I mean genuine, nurturing and healing of the mind, body, and spirit as opposed to more material or ego-based needs.

Optimally, we will see and address the err of our ways. We will grow and finally become self-referring relative to our sense of self worth, inner peace and happiness, and as we do that, ideally, like the prodigal son, our child will also see the err of their ways, acknowledge the new, self respecting, self reliant person we've become, along with our new boundaries and relationship standards, and return to us. Just bear in mind that you're dealing with a very strong E-generation personality who may still firmly believe in two former truths that they used to rely on heavily:

1) They run the show, not you.
2) You are there to love and serve them unconditionally as a Super-pleaser, fixer, enabler, rescuer, et al. On top of that, that you are at-the-ready for service as either a scapegoat or soft target.

Old habits, pride and *'being right'* are hard things to surrender, especially if the situation/abuse has existed for many years. Healthy and lasting change can only occur for those who truly desire and seek it. Bear in mind as you learn to respect yourself and set boundaries that growth and change occurs only with the passage of time; sometimes quickly as if by epiphany, but most times, slowly and with deliberate action. Also remember that *God's time* is not *our time*. Rest in the knowledge that all things happen at just the right time in life and also work for the ultimate good of all parties involved. This is the juncture where standing your ground in a spirit of love, faith, and patience plays a key role.

Defending the Fort—Keep your boundaries lovingly but firmly in place

I am not talking about responding to a polite text, email, card or call, nor am I suggesting that you cannot or should not extend an olive branch to those that have been less than kind to you. I am however, imploring you to make sure that you and your adult child, step-child, in-law are on the same page and that they are in full understanding and agreement with creating a new, healthy, and mutually honest and respectful relationship. If they are not there yet, then I believe it is incumbent upon you to lovingly, yet strongly maintain your boundaries in a spirit of self respect, patience, and love. But, as with all decisions of the heart, it is yours alone to make.

Patience is a virtue, both with your child and with yourself

There are parents out there who will share their feelings and needs, set boundaries, and have them instantly acknowledged and respected. We bless and envy them. To them I say—you are our inspiration because for many of us, it's going to be a much longer and much more harrowing path to travel. That is why we must be patient with ourselves and with our children. Accept in advance that you will have days when you're on top of the world and feeling very empowered and proud of yourself, and that there will also be days when you will barely be able to keep your chin up because you miss your child or grandchildren and feel that you're not making progress. Remember, you are not stubbornly standing your ground in defiance, insisting that you have everything *'your way.'* You are setting healthy boundaries relative to bad or abusive behavior and requiring mutual respect and cooperation in achieving shared respect and harmony. Once your boundaries have been established and you are in a healing place, you should stand ready with an open heart and open arms to reconcile with your family. As you pray and await reconciliation, recognize that there will be times when you will be tempted to go back to your pleaser/server/rescuer/fixer role. If and when that happens, I encourage you to take a personal tally of how many times you've done that over the course of your relationship and then ask yourself—what is the quality of a reconciliation under those conditions? Do I have to walk on egg shells in order to maintain peace? Historically, how long has the reconciliation lasted before abuse or neglect began again? In the past, how have I ultimately been treated when I respond in this way? And lastly, how will I feel about myself and my sense of self esteem, personal growth, or the violation of boundaries I've set if I do this?

Because you cannot control how long your child or their significant other *(if they're the one calling the shots)* will resist or refuse the respectful contact and relationship boundaries and goals you have established, it's important to acknowledge that fact and be patient with life's lessons, always remembering that there is a time to plant, a time to nurture and grow, a time to reap the harvest, and finally, a time to celebrate. You will have to trust that you have planted the seeds and that time, patience, personal growth *(yours and theirs)* along with God/spirit's guidance, accompanied by the sheer power of your love, will nurture that seed, and that one day you will all reap the harvest.

"Trust in the Lord *(*spirit/your higher power)* with all your heart.
Lean not onto your own understanding.
In all your ways, acknowledge him*
&
he shall direct your path."
Proverbs 3: 5-6

CHAPTER 18

Forgiveness, Healing & Reconciling in a Healthy Way

What if it Can't or Does Not Happen?

Healthy Healing & Reconciliation

There are no established rules for loving or for defining relationships. Human emotions and relationship dynamics are far too complex to be labeled or fit into neat little boxes; however, there are some essential elements that must be present in order for any relationship to sustain healthy love and flourish; those are:

- ❖ Emotional honesty and vulnerability (in word and deed)
- ❖ A commitment to personal integrity, which cultivates and encourages an atmosphere and ability to trust on the part of all parties.
- ❖ An authentic and deep mutual respect (in both word and deed). Realized/genuine respect is the shield that protects the participants of any relationship from emotional, financial, verbal or physical abuse or neglect.
- ❖ Living the reality that *healthy love* is not meant to be tested; it is not a game to be won, a battle to be fought, or a territory to be conquered or lorded over; nor is it meant to become one's personal life support system.

Think of all the healthy relationship qualities listed above as essential parts of a *whole*, and that whole is authentic, healthy reciprocal love.

You can certainly experience parts of the whole/love for another human being but whether it's healthy and sustainable is determined by the quality and wholeness of the love. An emotional attachment that does not contain the elements of love we noted above is not representative of whole, genuine, healthy love. It's been my experience and observation in life that if the essential elements of healthy love are missing or are not recognized and practiced in your relationship, you will experience pain and emptiness over time.

After speaking with dozens and dozens of parents in pain, I can only encourage you to establish some ground rules, set appropriate boundaries if there has been disrespectful or unhealthy behavior in the past or you're experiencing it presently. Communicate your love and desire for a healthy relationship that meets the standards and goals you've established for yourself, your life, and your relationships. Your child may respond in the positive; however, if you've previously allowed all manner of bad behavior to rule your life, then plan on digging your feet in the sand and prepare for the waves of resistance that may come crashing down upon you as your child resists you and attempts to resume power. This resistance may manifest itself in the form of overt negative behavior or via them withdrawing their love. Some adult children will choose to do this because they know that *their love and approval* has previously been the one thing you craved and needed the most and that threatening to take it away has worked rather effectively whenever you rocked the boat in the past.

If a battle has been waged on the part of your adult child, hold your ground and do not give up the fort. Although on its face, this may sound like a contradiction to the statement above that insisted that love is not war to be waged or a battle to be won. I assure you, it is not a contradiction in that what your adult child is exercising (and what you are resisting) is willfulness and power, not love. Love for yourself and for your child is what you are taking a stand for, so stay in that healthy place. If war has been declared by your child (not you) and a battle for power and control ensues, you must stand your ground—this is the ultimate act of love. Being competitive with an ex, using children or grandchildren as weapons, pawns or for leverage, dominating a partner or child, these are examples of love being viewed as a battle ground, something to be conquered, won or lost. They are also examples of how love should *not* behave itself. To take a stand against the ongoing manipulation, drama, and pain that is destroying your relationship while offering and supporting the establishment of new and healthy boundaries and goals is love in action; it is *respect* finally manifesting itself in your life.

With healthy love, grace and determination guiding you, establish your boundaries and work to create a healthy relationship with your child, a place where you can both experience love in a respectful way that does not use or denigrate another. If you identify unhealthy aspects of yourself and your relationship, set boundaries and establish goals for yourself, but if your adult child does not respond positively to your desire to transform your life and relationships, what then?

When healing and reconciliation don't happen—Lovingly taking a time-out and giving your child space—Releasing your child to life and their higher power

Sometimes, in spite of your best efforts, or maybe because of them, you may not (at least for the moment or on the surface) appear to be succeeding in your desire to create a loving, healthy, respectful, and reciprocal bond with your adult child. This is the time to remember that your child is an adult, and that even if you did everything 99% right they still may reject you, your values, and lifestyle. Your adult child's behavior may defy logic, boggle your mind, and break your heart as your try to understand why you're in this lonely state of pain and isolation. What did you do wrong? Why doesn't your child offer you the love and respect you feel you have earned and deserve? The same love and respect you've always given to them. Perhaps they call you only when they need something or maybe you spend your birthdays and holidays alone, sad, and grieving. It's just not right, is it? Let me say it for you, no, it is not fair and it most certainly is not the *right thing* to do to a loving and thoughtful parent; on top of that, it's excruciatingly painful. I am sorry you are experiencing this sadness and pain, but remember—sometimes life is not fair. Also remember that God's time is <u>not</u> *our time.* If your adult child is blatantly disrespectful, abusive, dangerous, or has rejected you altogether, that may indicate that it's time to forgive and lovingly release them (give them time and space) to receive the lessons they must learn in life. As important as setting boundaries and releasing your child in order to allow them to learn life's lessons without you constantly there to pick up the pieces or shout in their ear, is authentically forgiving them.

You can and must learn, and then practice the art of forgiveness because the only person you hurt by holding onto an emotional wound or grudge is you.

Mark Twain expressed a beautiful truth about forgiveness when he wrote:

> *"Forgiveness is the fragrance the violet sheds on the heel that crushed it."*

The Wilderness Experience

Imagine your life's journey as a hike in the woods, an expedition into new beginnings, endings, new lessons, experiences of all kinds, peaks, valleys, concessions, decisions, triumphs and tragedies all designed to help you grow spiritually; a passage from one stage of development to another. On this trek in the wilderness, you stop and smell the many beautiful and fragrant flowers along the path. You encounter breathtaking beauty and amazing spectacles on your journey, and your heart soars with joy. You also experience pit-falls along the way. Consider that every time you experienced an injustice, hurt or injury on your journey, it manifests as a stone. Sometimes you encounter small, unnoticeable stones, or pebbles. Other times it's a rock you step over, taking it in stride. But sometimes, sometimes hurt and pain manifest as larger stones that stop you in your tracks and hinder your progress along the path or as a bolder that rolls down unexpectedly on you and blocks your path entirely. There will most assuredly be those pebbles and small stones that you'll take in your stride perhaps hardly even noticing them, let alone allowing them to curtail your journey, but then comes the bigger hurts/bigger stones. If the hurt comes from a trusted intimate (spouse, sibling or child) then the stone is massive, dense, and incredibly heavy. A stone that big and imposing would represent a major impasse on your path; a hindrance that holds the potential of making an otherwise enjoyable, tranquil, and successful journey quite a challenge, if not a downright torture or impossible. But, lucky for you, on this journey, while you travel this path, you possess the power to make one of three choices whenever you came upon a stone that blocks your path.

The Three Choices Offered Along the Path

One—you could feel the pain of the stone's impact, be open to the lesson it came to teach, thank it for its appearance *(remembering that when the student is ready the teacher will appear)* and then remove the stone from your path or make your way around it while receiving its lesson and healing any wounds you received from it. You would then proceed merrily on your way, having learned something of value, even if it's patience and forgiveness, or simply how to better anticipate and navigate the twists and turns life offers along your journey through it to the other side.

Two—You could become so angry and so indignant over your hurt (real or perceived) that you become obsessed with the stone that inflicted the pain and consequently cannot get around it. And why should you want to? After all, the unmitigated gall of that stone to injure you, an innocent traveler along life's path. The choice is yours—you could remove or move past the stone or you can sit with it and obsess about it (experiencing the pain of that impact over and over again while making yourself and everyone around you miserable). If you make this choice, just know that you are inadvertently choosing NOT to progress any further on your journey because you're choosing to *get stuck.*

If we are not open, mature or enlightened enough to select option one, but tell ourselves that we do not want to remain stuck on the path with option two because we are feel we can move forward while at the same time maintaining our unwillingness or inability to move past the stone, we select option three.

Three—You want to move ahead or at least, *look* like you're moving ahead and making progress, but you can't let go of the stone; you can't forgive or even put a practical or spiritual context or understanding around your encounter with the stone—you just cannot let it go! So what do you do with the stone? You pick it up and carry it with you along the trail. That way you can tell yourself that you're moving along the path/you're making the journey while reserving the right to take out your stone and contemplate it, yell at it, obsess about it, cry over it, and revisit the pain over and over again. And you don't just collect *'that stone'*—you collect them all! And the stones you collect along the path become your constant companions and eventually dictate the quality of your thoughts, emotions, life; they also inhibit the progress you make along the path. And sometimes, you're so tired from carrying the stones, or so distracted by their weight that you miss the beauty all around you as you struggle to maintain your footing on the trail. The whole purpose of the journey has been lost, paid as a ransom to your insistence on keeping and carrying these stones. You don't stop and smell the roses, watch the animals frolic and play, enjoy the scents, the scenery, the tranquility, the rainbow, instead all your attention and energy is focused on the load you're carrying.

These are just some of the sad side effects you'll experience. There are several more very bad, self-defeating side effects to carrying all these stones with you. The first one being that you cannot and will not ever heal from the original injury, let alone allow it to be your teacher because you're carrying the source of its pain with you and are routinely peeling off the scab and reopening the wound over and over again. Another detrimental side effect of deciding to carry all those heavy stones along with you on your path is that you will never be able to fully be present for or enjoy all the beautiful things there are to see, smell, and experience along the path. Saddest of all, you will not complete your journey but will slowly travel in painful circles. If option three is the choice you make on your journey, then recognize too that your chances of healing, learning, growing, and enjoying your journey are remote at best.

Lastly, and this is the most important thing to remember about this choice—if you can't let go of one stone, you'll never leave the others behind either. You will begin to hoard every stone that crosses your path. Imagine yourself on this wonderful nature trail, the hike that is your life. As we all do, you have encountered stones along the way, but rather than learning from the experience, removing them or simply navigating around them once you've learned what it is they've come to teach you, you keep them. By choosing not to learn the lesson when it's offered and then leave them in your past where they can no longer injure or hinder you, you have picked them up and put them in your backpack. What do you think happens if you decide to lug around a backpack full of heavy painful stones all your life? If you have any doubt, please, strap on a backpack, go to your nearest wildness trail or rock quarry and begin collecting stones and placing them in your backpack and see how far you get. Pretty soon, there's no room for anything but stones. There is no joy, there is no peace, and there is no progress. There is only pain and stagnation. Eventually, you can move no further and collapse under the weight of your own burden—the burden of a continued commitment to victimhood and un-forgiveness.

A wonderful and beneficial side effect of forgiveness is that it serves you before it serves its recipient. Whenever you make the decision to hold onto a hurt by not exercising forgiveness and moving forward, I want you to imagine it as choosing to carry a heavy stone on your back. What would that feel like? How long could you carry it and what effect would its burden have on you? Pick up a heavy rock and carry it with you constantly for a week, a day, or even an hour and actually experience how it feels to carry unnecessary weight in your life. If you think you'd look ridiculous and would never consider that *(after all, what would people think?)* then consider what you're carrying on your back and in your heart right now and how it's affecting every facet of your life and relationships, especially the one you have with yourself and your higher power. Let it go and continue on your life-path my friend. You have the choice. Choose to smell the sweet scent of the woods, listen instead to the singing of the birds, watch the animals at play, take in the fragrance of the violet you see crushed along the path, and when you come upon a stone that injures you, learn from the experience, heal and be thankful for it, and then remove it or navigate your way past that experience. Do not pick the stone up and make it your companion along life's journey. I promise, you will be the better for it.

Remember my friend Jennifer? She is the wonderful woman whose tragic death inspired this book. She picked up so many painful stones along her path, and she struggled to carry them all. She hid them away so others couldn't see the burden she labored under. But finally, after one too many birthdays alone, one too many Christmas's spent in pain and solitude, she could no longer bear the burden of those painful stones. Her burden was far too heavy and my friend collapsed under the weight of the pain she'd been carrying on her shoulders and in her heart for so many years, and when she did, she was crushed by it. Jennifer's burden and pain ultimately cost her, her life. Please, do not carry all this woundedness inside you. Let it go, forgive, grow, and give back. If you feel that you simply cannot forgive, then practice the *willingness* to forgive, and if it's beyond you to do that, if you're crumbling under the burden of the stones you've chosen to carry on your shoulder and in your heart, please find someone to help you identify and remove the stones so you can get back on your path and back to the trail and all its delights.

For those of you for whom, circumstances cannot or will not *change (death, imprisonment, prolonged estrangement or abandonment)*

I do not pretend to have all the answers to these sorrowful situations but will share from my own experience and those of other parents who have been in the midst of this pain and have managed to move beyond it.

Loss via substance abuse, crime, or prison

Losing a child to a criminal lifestyle, gangs, drugs, or to prison is a pain and social stigma that many parents endure. It is a pain tangibly different from, yet in some limited ways, akin to the loss of death. Ask a parent who has an adult child sitting on death row and you may begin to understand their sense of loss. It was surprising to me, how many parents said they'd be more at peace if their child were killed in an auto accident as opposed to being irrevocably lost to gangs, drugs, or sentenced to death row. When a son or daughter's mind and future is lost (for example, to drugs or alcohol) it has a similar impact as death because the person's essence, their very being, is gone and only the shell of a person remains. To watch such self-destruction play itself out in the life of one's child as they commit passive suicide is an agony every parent hopes never to suffer, yet sadly, many do. Many parents who have endured this kind of trauma and loss, have reclaimed and enriched their lives by helping others, connecting with other parents, and by becoming a force for healing and good in their families and communities.

Prolonged estrangement—total abandonment

Like other forms of loss, involuntary estrangement is hard to wrap one's mind and heart around and make peace with, especially for good parents who did not initiate and do not understand why they've been evicted from their adult-child's life. With death or an adult child's election to immerse themselves in a life of crime, drugs, alcohol or some other debilitating lifestyle choice, there is an explanation for the loss, and believe it or not, a lot of parents, say that knowing there is cause and effect in action or something or someone to blame, makes it more palatable for them, not acceptable or less painful, just intellectually palatable. When an adult child takes their love away or abandons their parent, and there is no logical explanation or catalyst that the parent is aware of or can decipher, the wound stays open and resists healing because there is no explanation, no context around which to understand what's happened, no closure. Conversely, when a parent attempts a healthy intervention with the adult child, seeking to set boundaries and establish a healthy relationship and the child rejects that opportunity and the parent(s) take a time out in response, again, there is a context around which the estrangement has occurred, and in that instance, there is a olive branch extended to the adult child at all times, should they decide to rein in the offending behavior and respect the reasonable boundaries and healthy relationship goals established by their parent(s).

Death

Death is the ultimate form of permanent tangible human loss. I call it tangible because I truly believe (and know within my own soul) that the spirit does go on, that it is indestructible. The tangible body can be lost, but the soul goes on. I have experienced a great deal of death in my own life, and for me, I liken death to having a beloved friend or relative move to a distant land where there is virtually no means of communication. You know they're there. You know they're safe. You know they're not in pain and enjoying a state of bliss, yet you are sad and lonely for them because you can't see them, touch them, or talk to them anymore. Having shared my personal views about what most people call *death* and I call *transition*, I also know that *talk is cheap* and analogies are easy to make but losing someone you love brings with it an indescribable pain and a loss that defies definition, especially when it is your child who's been lost. There is no greater pain than to lose a child because inherent in a parent's rudimentary belief system is the notion that they will not outlive their children and grandchildren, and to do so ushers in an ever-present/everlasting pain to an already grieving heart; a pain and sorrow that may experience some form of healing and transition as time goes on, but will never completely go away.

Finding solace and support in your surviving children, your spouse, work, friends, extended family, community, and in your faith is critical. Relying on one's faith is a powerful ally in the battle for your serenity and the return of happiness and purpose in life. If you do not possess a strong and abiding faith, establishing a relationship with your higher power (however you define it) and allowing whatever peace you derive from it to carry you through is

175

essential. Another tool that many parents of lost children utilize is grief counseling and support groups.

Important Note—With the epidemic of child abductions in this country, I would be remiss in not speaking to those parents and their pain. They experience not only the same emotions as parents who have lost a child to death, but in addition to that, they experience the never-ending agony of not knowing for sure what happened to their child. For these parents, life and their very emotions become a cruel and sadistic mixture of hope, horror, and pain. The same therapies recommended to the parents of children who have died is recommended to this very special group of grieving parents. Our thoughts and our prayers are with you always.

Ellen's Story

Ellen lived in Seattle, Washington. She had two sons: Jonathan and Gregory. The boys were two years apart in age and she loved them dearly. Ellen and her husband went through a divorce when the boys were twelve and fourteen. Shortly after the divorce, Ellen was offered an incredible job in Miami, Florida. It was a once in a lifetime opportunity that Ellen felt she must take advantage of it. Her ex-husband and sons were adamant, the boys would not leave Washington, and the courts agreed. Ellen, was wounded but nonetheless, made the move south and began her new career, seeing the boys whenever she could. Ellen was often plagued with guilt and soon after her move, depression set in. Assuring herself that she'd made the right decision, the *only* decision available to her in so far as supporting herself went, Ellen moved forward with her life and career and planned on seeing the boys that summer.

It was Easter weekend when Ellen got a call informing her that there had been a terrible car accident. Her husband's entire family had been caravanning in multiple vehicles, all heading to the mountains for a holiday picnic when Ellen's sister-in-law lost control of her car and went careening over a mountain pass. Gregory, Ellen's youngest son, his aunt, and three of his cousins *(his best friends)* were killed instantly. Ellen was devastated. She could not accept that she would never see her youngest son again. The pain was excruciating and unrelenting. What if she had stayed? Gregory would never have been in the car with his aunt; he would have traveled with her. Ellen took what solace she could from the fact that her eldest son, Jonathon was traveling in another car and had survived.

Losing a child creates an absolutely incomprehensible pain and loss that cuts to the very soul of a parent; a pain none of us can imagine. Whatever depression and guilt Ellen experienced surrounding her divorce and subsequent move was minuscule compared to what she experienced after the loss of her son Gregory. Her older son, Jonathon, Jon as he liked to be called, enjoyed an extraordinarily close relationship with his little brother and was distraught by his sudden death. Ellen was beside herself with constant worry for her surviving son and wanted him by her side. Because Jonathon missed his brother so desperately and needed his mother's love, strength and support, his father agreed to let him move to Florida to live with her. Ellen was grateful to her ex-husband for making what must have been a heartbreaking decision. Like Ellen, Gregory's father was suffering tremendous guilt and was feeling responsible for their youngest son's death. No matter how unwarranted, he felt he had failed and now owed it to the mother of his surviving son to allow her to watch over him.

Jonathon acclimated quickly to life in Florida and easily made friends at the high school he was enrolled in shortly after his arrival. Ellen pampered and spoiled her son. She also worried to excess about him. Ellen never got over Gregory's death, with the effect being that she watched over Jonathan like a prison guard. When it came time for him to get his license, she begrudgingly allowed it but refused to get him a car. Feeling that no harm could come to her son if she was there to watch over him, Jonathon was not allowed to drive without his mother beside him in the car. Ellen would escort her son to school dances and parties, and never allowed him to travel without her. Ellen became a loving but paranoid *smother mother*. Her worry and hovering began to suffocate her son, but, to his credit, Jonathan loved his mother and understood where her fear and concern came from.

High school flew by and before they knew it Jonathan was graduating with honors. His father came down for the ceremony. To Ellen's utter shock and dismay, his graduation gift to his son was a new car. Jonathan's father invited him to spend the summer with him in Washington before heading off to college. Jonathan had spent summers with his dad since his move to Florida but the trips always made his mother uneasy. She would call him daily to check in on him, sometimes several times a day. Considering the anxiety it would cause his mother, Jonathan was tempted to decline his father's offer and stay home for the summer. He also reasoned that in addition to pleasing his mother, he could prepare for college and buzz around town in his new car. He seemed to have more reasons to stay than to go, but in the end, Jonathan didn't want to appear unappreciative to his father or imply that he didn't want to spend one last summer with him. Looking on the bright side, Jonathan loved Seattle and knew it might be the last summer he'd have to spend with his family and childhood friends.

Jonathan would be gone for a month. Ellen was nervous and uneasy about the trip from the start, but then she was always that way whenever Jon went anywhere without her. To soothe her nerves, Ellen would call Jonathan daily, sometimes twice a day, and he never objected. Three weeks into his visit, Jonathan and his friends were heading to the rocky coasts of Washington to spend a boys night out fishing. Knowing that he wouldn't be home in time to receive his mother's routine 10am phone call the following morning (this was before cell phones) Jonathan called his mother to tell her he was going out for the evening and would talk to her the following afternoon. Ellen was not home when Jonathan called so he left a message on her answering machine. After arriving home and retrieving the message, Ellen was relieved and grateful for her son's thoughtfulness in calling. The happiness and confidence in his voice was contagious and Ellen went to bed and slept soundly for the first time since he left Florida. Then, just as it had before, the phone rang in the dark, wee hours of the night. Awaking in terror, Ellen immediately shot a glance at the digital clock beside her bed and did not want to answer the phone but knew she must when she saw on the digital display that it was an incoming call from Washington.

Trembling, her heart pounding in her chest, Ellen picked up the receiver. The voice on the other end of the phone was barely audible as it struggling through deep sighs and tears to speak. *"Jonathan is dead Ellen!"* cried the quivering voice at the other end of the line. Did you hear me Ellen? *"Our Jonathan is dead . . ."* Jonathan, just seventeen years old, and the second son to die, had been killed in an auto accident.

Jonathan and his three best friends had been traveling to the coast when a heavy fog set in and overtook the narrow mountain roads. Jonathan, who was behind the wheel when the accident occurred, was not an experienced driver and had improperly navigated a turn in the dense fog. The vehicle carrying the four boyhood friends flew blindly off the mountain road and down a deep precipice, flipping over and over until it came to rest in a creek at the bottom of the ravine. Like his brother before him, Jonathan was killed along with his three best friends. Mixed with, and over-lapping the nightmarish scenes in her head were memories of her youngest son's tragic death. Distraught, overwhelmed, and numb with a combination of shock and disbelief, the surreal nightmare would play itself out over and over in Ellen's mind as she prepared for the trip to Seattle. Ellen bravely told me that after the call, she simply could not believe that God would take both her boys in identical accidents, and each with their three best friends. Ellen firmly believed that it was some kind of horrible mistake and that Jonathan was still alive. She said she would not believe it until she saw his body with her own eyes. Ellen sobbed uncontrollable as she told me that she had deleted Jonathan's last phone message the night before because she was so sure she would speak to her son the next afternoon. With her head buried in my shoulder, Ellen cried over and over *"I'll never get to hear my son's voice again."* The story of a mother who loses both her sons in nearly identical accidents three years apart is completely unimaginable and almost unbelievable, and yet, it is tragically true. The pain for Ellen was insurmountable, or so it seemed for a very long time.

I share this unbelievably heartbreaking story not to tug at your heart strings or emotionally manipulate you, but to proclaim and celebrate the incredible courage of this remarkable woman. Even in the depths of a loss and a sorrow that we can never imagine, and pray never to experience, Ellen found the courage and strength she needed to hang on, even when it was a thin thread of hope that she clung to. Ellen got herself into therapy and then bought herself a puppy to love and care for. As an ancillary means of support, Ellen spent a period of time on meds to help her manage the shock and devastation of her loss. But more important than that, Ellen didn't give up on herself, even though many times, she was tempted to quit on life and '*join her sons*' (as she put it). Something inside her said *no*. Somewhere in her wounded heart, she found the insight and courage to intuitively know that, to quit on herself or life was *not* the right choice to make because it would not honor her sons lives or her own. Ellen leaned heavily on her faith and became determined to transform her pain and suffering into an opportunity to grow and to help others. That was fifteen years ago. Today, to see the joy Ellen exudes and the love she so freely gives to everyone around her is her gift to this world. I am sure she feels the loss of her boys daily and has never tried to diminish or deny it; she has however, transformed its energy into something positive and powerful. Ellen made the decision to celebrate her son's lives as well as her own by becoming a force for good in her life and in the lives of others. Ellen worked hard at getting well and balanced; she also worked diligently to become a doctor, and not just any kind of doctor, a doctor who would bring life into the world. That made all the difference for Ellen. She became a force for good, for healing, and for life itself. Ellen had her primary source of love tragically taken from her but decided out of sheer force of will, not only to survive but to create a world where she could again experience love, contribution, and joy.

If Ellen could do with it with the loss and challenges she experienced in life then we can do it too. Most of us cannot, in our most hellish nightmares imagine the pain and loss Ellen experienced, but we do know about our own, and if you hold it up against Ellen's and it doesn't measure up, be thankful. Also, begin to acknowledge and appreciate what you *do have* in your life. And if like Ellen, you may not be able to eliminate a painful event, circumstance or condition in your life or make a profound loss disappear, but recognize that what you can do is make the brave and bold decision to add a layer of love and meaning to your life experience, and then another, and another, and another . . . and you can do that for the rest of your life.

The Five Stages of Grief as applied to a free mom to good home

1. Denial and Isolation
   Whether you have suffered the loss of a loved-one through death or as the result of alcohol, drug use, prison, estrangement, or runaway, you will experience all five stages of grief to one degree or another. You may deny that the loss has occurred or is even real. You may hide it from friends and other family members. You may withdraw from your usual social contacts. This painful stage of grief can last anywhere from days to months. For some, it can go on for years.

2. Anger
   In time, grief gives way to episodes of anger or resentment. As a grieving parent, you may become intensely upset with the adult child, person or situation you feel is responsible for the suffering or the injustices you feel have been heaped upon you. Once this parasitical virus takes over a person's life, it becomes easy to get mad and blame the whole world and even God (for letting it happen). Many times, we mothers become most angry at ourselves and beat ourselves up for allowing the unhealthy situation to develop and flourish, even if there was nothing we could do about it.

3. Bargaining
   A grieving parent may attempt to bargain with God/the Universe. I'll *do this*, or I'll *stop doing that*, if you'll only _____ (fill in the blank). A typical example would be *'I promise I'll stop smoking if you'll only deliver my child from cancer.'* The bargaining chip may be giving up a vice, attending church more regularly, etc. but at the end of the day, bargaining with God does not work, it only delays the

inevitable work one must do in order to get past one's pain and grow.

4. <u>Depression</u>

Once grief, denial and anger have exhausted themselves, and bargaining has failed, the grieving mother will often feel disconnected, numb, and as if life has lost its purpose, especially if she singularly defined herself via her role of mother and then lost it. If the depression is transient and manageable, it can be worked through, if it becomes overbearing and life has lost its purpose and vitality, then it's time to seek help.

5. <u>Acceptance</u>

When the loss is permanent, acceptance is the last stage in the grieving process. However, when there are other/transient relationship dynamics that have created a temporary loss and grief state, hope for healing and reconciliation will naturally remain. That hope aside, accepting where you are in the process is important. Work on accepting that *'this is how life is right now'* while appreciating that it may not always be this way. Today is the gift you can hold and embrace now, and now is the time you can begin to take back ownership of your life. That is what Ellen did. Whether your children are alive or deceased, present in your life or estranged from you, remember—hope and love are still available to you.

Humans are the only species who can create love
where once there was none.
and miraculously,
we can do it at will, simply because we decide to.

CHAPTER 19

Forget the Four Letter Word
It's the 8-Letter Word that can Hurt the Most

The Holidays!

This chapter presupposes that you've lost a relationship permanently or are currently estranged from one or more of your children or other significant family members and are consequently spending the holidays sad and alone. Time is a wastin'—Christmas is comin' and there's no use crying over spilt eggnog, so let's start in the fall.

Halloween

Ignoring costume parties and the consumption of large quantities of candy seems survivable enough, it's the little ghosts and goblins arriving at the door that can be painful, especially for grandparents estranged from their adult children and not allowed to see their grandchildren on the holidays. If it makes you feel better to be around little ones, then buy loads of candy and enjoy, if not, Halloween is one of the easiest holidays to avoid/survive emotionally. Just don't be at home to open the door. Go out to dinner or to the movies.

Thanksgiving

Ah, *Turkey Day*—that's a biggie! It's also a time of year when lonely, sensitive people can sink into deep depression. This happens with seasonal regularity because our culture tells us via all media sources that we are supposed to be connected to family and experience the holidays with them. If we are not a member of the club then there's something woefully wrong with poor ole pathetic us; at least, that's what we tell ourselves, hence the long lines at the therapist's office from November through the new year. You'll notice that no advice or helpful anecdotes have been doled out for Thanksgiving. *"What's the deal?"* you're wondering. Well, so as *not* to be redundant, I'm throwing all the holidays, including two of the biggest, most emotionally charged liabilities/holidays (Christmas & Hanukkah) into one cursory bunch and will later offer the bulk of holiday survival advice when we reach Easter, and then more when we get to the biggest of them all, the mack-daddy of all holidays and the holy grail for mothers.

Christmas & Hanukkah

Again, according to established societal standards and expectations, these are holidays that are meant to be spent with one's family. These two holidays come complete with the same rejection theory, and policies that apply to Thanksgiving, and that is: if you're not included, you are either the black sheep or somehow socially inferior. Any way you slice it, these holidays, when spent alone, can produce a profound sense of loss and disconnection which often produces deep depression for persons without family or who may be temporarily or permanently estranged from their children and/or other family members this time of year. Again, remember that we're going to address specifics when we reach the big mystery holiday I alluded to earlier. But for now, know that if you make it through Christmas and Hanukkah in one piece, you can celebrate your victory on December 31st

New Year's Eve

New Year's Eve is celebrated differently around the nation, and indeed, the world. For some families, it's a time to stay close, while for others, it's a time to get as far away as you can and party with your friends. It does not rank high on the list of emotionally volatile holidays for wounded parents and grandparents who must spend it without their children or grandchildren; however, the day after (January 1ˢᵗ) may be, as many families have New Year's Day traditions they cherish. For my family is was plopping in front of the television and watching the Tournament of Roses Parade on TV. If you have a family tradition you're accustomed to upholding, invite friends to celebrate with you or change it up a bit and do something different.

Martin Luther King Day

Depending on how your family celebrates, you may feel alone and sad or you may hold your own on this nationally celebrated holiday. Some holidays have become synonymous with 'family.' Many of the African American families I interviewed, cherish Martin Luther King Day as day to celebrate family and kinship, as well as a day to observe and honor the civil rights movement and one of its greatest architects, as should all Americans regardless of their skin color. If it is not possible to celebrate with family, find some friends, enjoy one of the many parades that celebrate the day and our on-going journey towards total equality.

Valentine's Day

If Martin Luther King Day is meant to celebrate an incredible man's life and the search for equality, then Valentine's Day is all about the search for romantic love. While traditionally celebrated by lovers, there are many parents who send cards or gifts to their children or grandchildren and may feel left out or sad. Remember, you can always put cards into keepsake chests like Cindy does. My advice is that you lavish your attention on your lover, or absent a partner, celebrate Valentine's Day by lavishing love upon yourself, you deserve it. Demonstrate your new self esteem and self respect by doing something nice for yourself on Valentine's Day.

St. Patrick's Day

St Patrick's Day is notably *not* a family celebration day, that is, unless you're Irish American. Generally speaking, it's a day for the *'wearing of the green'* and like New Year's Eve, it's holiday designated for and dedicated to the pursuit of drinking and partying; and in some culinary quarters, to the consumption of corned beef and cabbage along with alcohol. If you love St. Paddy's Day and traditionally celebrate with family, get focused on what you enjoy most about it, ring up some friends or make some friends when you visit your local Irish Pub. Sing some Irish songs, dance an Irish jig, listen to the bag pipes, eat some corned beef and cabbage, drink responsibly, and celebrate the life and friends you do have, and whatever you do, don't forget to wear green.

Easter *(and the other big family holidays)*

As our children become teens and then into the adult years, most parents who celebrate the holiday usually don't get baskets or gifts or hide eggs for their children once they're grown up. Most families do, however, share dinner, and if there are grandchildren, then all the customary childhood rituals are observed. Like Thanksgiving, Christmas and Hanukkah, Easter is designated as a *'family holiday'* and therefore can be tough to face alone. What I did one year when I knew I'd be alone was: first, realize that other people must also feel alone and craved company on the holidays too. That being the case, I threw a holiday orphan's dinner. Social media made it easy to announce my invitation to any of my friends who were going to be alone for the holidays. What was destined to be a lonely and sad day for me, ended up being one the best holidays ever. I had six friends thankfully communicate their joy and relief at being invited to do something on the holiday. I made up care baskets filled with things I thought each friend would enjoy and together we all celebrated and thoroughly enjoyed what could have been a very lonely and isolated day for many of us.

Whether it's Christmas, Hanukkah, or Easter, you can create a loving or celebratory atmosphere for yourself and others if you really want to and are committed to creating that experience for yourself. You can elect to do something completely different than what you're accustomed to. Whether you plan a get-together for friends or attend one as a guest, you have choices. You can go mountain biking, golfing, sky-diving, parasailing, hiking, spend the day at the ocean, take a long walk on the beach, read a good book, volunteer, go see a movie, go on a cruise—the choices are a vast as your imagination. Just do something that is so wildly different that it breaks up the pattern of emotions and expectations that you're accustomed to feeling on that day. By replacing those emotions and expectations with a new and unfamiliar experience, you are focusing you thoughts and emotions in a direction they're not acquainted with, that makes them less likely to wander into the realm of familiar expectations or emotions affixed to that particular holiday.

The Mack Daddy of holidays for moms—**MOTHER'S DAY**

There are three hundred and sixty-five days in the year, and one of them is set aside just for you. On May 8, 1914 President Woodrow Wilson signed a joint resolution designating the second Sunday in May as *Mother's Day*. After that, Hallmark and the restaurant industry jumped on board, and in an act of marketing genius decided that in addition to a day off from cooking and cleaning, mom also deserved a nice card and a gift to commemorate the day. Wow! Our own special day to get a nice card, perhaps a gift, but foremost, a day to take a vacation from cooking, and hopefully be thoroughly pampered by those who love, acknowledge, and appreciate us. I humorously prefer to think of *Mother's Day* as a day of worship for the selfless human being known as *'Mom.'* After all she's only the person who created and sustained life from the fibers of her very being, then carried, gave birth to, raised, and endured the antics of the one sending the flowers or buying her dinner at the Red Lobster, but that's just me. All attempts at humor aside, this holiday can be a very painful twenty-four hour period for those of us who have lost children or still have them but have been tossed out onto the highway and walk that lonely stretch of hot asphalt alone on Mother's Day. My advice for Mother's Day is pretty much the same as it is for Thanksgiving, Christmas/Hanukkah or Easter-stop buying into the cultural standard that says these holidays *must* be celebrated in such and such manner and with such and such persons. *"Baloney!"*—I say. Now I know what you're thinking; you're thinking *it's easier to say that about the other holidays, but Mother's Day too?'* After all, it is called *"MOTHER'S DAY"* for a reason. Yes, ideally we are meant to be loved, acknowledged, and hopefully pampered by our husbands and children on this day, but, just because it's called 'Mother's Day' does not mean that if circumstances do not permit such a celebration, you are emotionally and culturally enslaved by that label and must feel *less-than* or *left-out* on the second Sunday of May. Here's some advice from the painful trenches of experience. First, have a support system on hand *(partner, friends, plans, activities, etc)*. Second, do not, I repeat DO NOT buy into the whole line of bull that tells Americans how we are *supposed* to feel and how we are *supposed* to celebrate certain dates on the calendar. If you think of the holidays as a loaded gun, the best/most practical advice is—take out the freakin' bullets! Disable the gun and make it powerless in your life. You disable/dis-empower them by transforming the meaning of, and the way you celebrate those holidays by creating your own special traditions, values, and meanings for each holiday or by re-defining them as nothing more than *dates on a calendar*. Remember, the *power* and *meaning* that a person, place or things has over you, *you* give it. Whatever definition I give to an event, becomes the event. Whatever meaning I give to an event, becomes its meaning in my life, a meaning I then become bound to, so why not create a positive, empowering meaning?

When I faced my first Mother's Day estranged from a child I adored and had spent my life tirelessly working to please, serve and rescue when need be, I knew it would be rough on me. My husband and I originally planned on going to Disney World to keep me busy, but the night before, I changed my mind. I had been inundated with a media blitz of reminders of Mother's Day and it hurt. Television ads depicted loving displays of mothers receiving adulation, flowers, and love from their children; for me, it was gut-wrenching and heartbreaking. It was a constant reminder of what I *was not going to experience* and it hurt enormously. But, rather than indulge myself in a pity party, I decided that I needed to get away from the television and radio; away from the city and all the restaurants and theme parks filled with mothers adorned in corsages and ensconced by throngs of familial worshipers. Instead of choosing an environment ripe with Mother's Day reminders, we went out and spent the day on the Gulf of Mexico. When I was asked by my husband what I wanted for Mother's Day, I surprised him by saying *"A paddle board and a day on the water."* We busted the bank and bought two.

Why paddle boarding, well, it was something new and totally foreign to me, and it was an endeavor I knew would keep both my physical and emotional attention focused and in a positive place for the day. So while other mothers were being wined and dined, my husband and I spent the day trying in vain to stand up and stay atop paddle boards in the Gulf of Mexico. It was a new and exhilarating experience that required a complete commitment from me. My attention and emotions were held captive and could not wander off into unhealthy territory. In fact, we were *so busy* paddling to a nearby sandbar, collecting shells, swimming, and trying to stay atop our paddle boards that I hardly noticed that, for the rest of the world, it was *'Mothers Day.'* For me, it was *'Kay's Day'* and an *"Us"* day.

What would have otherwise been a sad and lonely day for me became an exceptional day because I proactively made the decision to redefine what the day meant to me and how I would spend it. I took back my power and decided for myself what I *would* and *would not* make it *mean* to me. I changed my label, expectation and focus and that changed my experience. You can do the same thing, no matter the holiday or its label. You can turn the television off, put on your favorite music and dance or sing along to it. You can go camping or on a wilderness walk or hike; golf, cycle, garden, take a Sunday drive or donate some time to a charity that speaks to your heart. The possibilities are as endless as your imagination and your determination to create a positive experience for yourself.

Memorial Day—Labor Day—the 4th of July

These holidays are almost always celebrated with family or friends and include traditional holiday staples such as outdoor sports, getting wet (either at the beach or by hose, pool, slip & slide, squirt guns or water balloons) libations and barbecuing. If you're accustomed to having a big family reunion or gathering, then seek out the company of friends and family that are supportive and will make your day a good experience rather than a sad one. Reach out and invite others who may also be alone to share the day with you. Absent a desire or the ability to do that, you can always redefine what that day means to you (or doesn't) and creatively choose another way to spend it.

Grandparents Day

For those of you who don't know or remember—Grandparent's Day falls on the second Sunday of September and can be especially painful for grandparents, who, by no fault of their own, can't spend the day with their grandchildren or perhaps don't even have a relationship with them. The same input, advice, and ideas given throughout this chapter are applicable here too. One note for grandparents—there are mentoring and fostering programs that you can join, and in doing so, have the experience of being there for a child and enriching their life, as well as your own.

Important Anniversaries

Like birthdays, important anniversaries are yet another potentially painful and challenging day to get through. Creating new and positive traditions and routines is a powerful way to use these milestones in life as a force for healing and good. If you cannot simply redefine the meaning of the day and lessen its impact by taking meaning *away* from the anniversary and its meaning, then do the opposite, then *add* meaning to the day; just be sure to add new and positive meaning and rituals. Find relevance in the event associated with that day and go out and do something that will honor that event, memory or person. For example, the day that my son was gravely injured in an auto accident and clung by the thinnest, most frailest thread of hope to life, was a significant date to me, as were the weeks that followed and his ultimate discharge date from the hospital. On the anniversary of his accident, the memories would flood back and often overwhelm me until I decided to break the pattern I had established. I decided that I would visit the trauma unit of the hospital and take with me goodies and thank you cards for the staff. I also wrote a book about the experience. These things helped me turn a traumatic event and it's memory into a healing and positive event with new/positive memories linked to the old painful ones. And, it honored the participants as well, making it a powerful replacement for the original meaning attached to the date of my son's accident. When facing an important anniversary, whether it's a cherished memory of good times or a tragic date that denotes loss and pain, take all that energy and funnel into a positive direction, use it as a force for good in your life and in the lives of others.

Birthdays

Whether it is your birthday or your son or daughters, it's a day packed with emotions; some worn on your sleeve and others buried deep inside you. We feel unloved, lonely, and unwanted when we spend our birthdays by ourselves, uncelebrated. And when we're out of sorts with our adult child and don't get to celebrate their birthday with them, ironically we feel the exact same way, unloved, lonely, and unwanted.

Your Child's Birthday

You can do what Cindy did and create special place to deposit notes, cards and gifts you hope to one day share with your child or grandchild. You can reach out to them without expectations (hoping for reconciliation and acceptance but prepared for rejection). You can volunteer to help others on that day, set a new personal goal to achieve on that day, plant a tree or a garden in honor of the love you have for your child and tend to it on each birthday that follows or you can simply treat birthdays as a day to remember good times and celebrate life itself in whatever way you define it.

Your Birthday

You have all kinds of option here. Because you are learning to heal, honor and appreciate yourself, this is the perfect day to do something positive for yourself or to volunteer to help others. The point to remember is—you have options. You possess the ability and power to redefine what certain days do or do not mean to you, as well as what significance and power they have relative to your happiness and sense of balance and peace. Don't give that power away, it's yours, keep it and celebrate it.

CHAPTER 20

Learning to Love, Honor & Nurture Yourself

Establishing a Genuine Sense of Self Esteem, Self Worth & Self Love

Think of the love you need as a lifeline, as your very life-source. Now, visualize the love you need and desire as a very specific type of food, your favorite food. You absolutely MUST eat that food in order to feel loved, nourished, thrive, and stay alive. Let's assume, for the purpose of this lesson, that your life-saving/life enriching food is bread, and not just any bread, oh no, you decided a long time ago that it could only be, must be *sourdough bread*. You have been hypnotized into believing that this particular type of bread is your only true source of life and nourishment and no other bread will suffice. If you have set your life up such that sourdough bread is the singular source of life and love for you, what happens if there a run on sourdough bread and it is no longer available to you? Poof, it's gone! What then? The answer is simple—you suffer the loss of your life source. And to the degree that you believe that sourdough bread alone is your true source of life sustaining nourishment and love, you will ignore all the other wonderful breads right in front of you, beckoning you. Many a famished heart would rather starve itself to death awaiting the return of its beloved sourdough before reaching for a warm slice of rye, whole grain, or perhaps sprouted-wheat; and God forbid they even entertain the notion of adding flat bread or a tortilla to their diet, that just wouldn't do. These hungry, misguided souls would rather wither away for want of their beloved sourdough than settle for what they perceive as *less than*. Sound familiar? Many people will ignore all other breads/sources of love and nourishment available to them as a response to their misplaced belief that the only bread that can give them the nourishment and love they need and crave is a sourdough alone. Crazy when you consider that there are dozens and dozens of wonderful, sumptuous breads to tantalize the taste buds and enjoy in life.

That's exactly what it's like for you when you make your children your singular/solitary reason for living—you're on a strict diet of motherhood and your only source of identity, love, happiness, and validation in life is fulfillment of that role as you've defined it. And just so you don't feel silly right about now, remember that you're not alone; most of us moms are guilty of attempting to define our lives and survive on this diet too. I believe that most women do this because at one time or another in their life they experienced a major let-down, disappointment, or outright betrayal by their parents, a sibling, trusted friend, husband or partner and that left a bad taste in their mouth and closed up their hearts (metaphorically speaking). The more betrayals a woman experiences in life, especially early on, the more likely it is that she will consciously or subconsciously entrust and anchor her love in one trusted source of love, her children, who she naively believes will never hurt her or betray her trust.

So what's a mother to do?

Don't put all your bread in one basket! And, don't put just one kind of bread in that basket either. It's okay to love your sourdough bread and recognize it as your very favorite food in all the world, but don't shortchange yourself and your future by believing that's it's the *only* bread that will keep you alive or that you can enjoy. And stop insisting on it alone when you can smell the sweet aroma of other breads that will enrich your diet and your life.

Pathways

Envision your heart as formerly having only one pathway leading into it for love to travel on. That sole pathway was your child's demonstration of love, approval and validation of you. When, for whatever reason, that conduit is blocked or severed, your heart is suddenly cut off from its only source of love (or so it is perceived); consequently, it becomes a lonely, dark, vacuum. You no longer have control over how you feel emotionally because the single pathway/ source you had to experience love, peace, validation, and joy in your life is now blocked. When this happens, the heart will suffocate and die.

Now picture your heart again but this time with multiple pathways, more than you can count. There is a glow around your heart and when you look more closely, you see something amazing and beautiful coursing in and out of your heart along those new pathways. It is flowing freely in all directions, glistening and luminescent. It is LOVE—the very love, peace, and joy you desire and deserve so much. Wow! Doesn't the mere thought and mental image of those luminescent pathways filled with love make your heart warm? It does mine.

How do we develop those pathways?

First, realize that although you love your sourdough bread and it has its place in your diet, you no longer need it alone to survive and thrive. The sourdough myth ends here and now! There is a big wide world out there and it's full of delectable delights for you to tantalize your emotional taste buds with, so stop depriving yourself! What you want and need is LOVE and connection. What you have done is construct a false reality in which the love you deserve, crave, and need in your life can only come from one source—your children. That is simply not true, not unless you decide to make it so. Love is always available to you. And if you don't see it right in front of you, know that you possess the unique privilege and honor of being the only species on planet earth that can simply decide to create love where none existed before. You, my friend have the inherent ability to create the healthy, reciprocal love you desire in your life. That is an amazing and wondrous miracle! Two humans can meet, spend time together, share common beliefs and experiences, form a bond, and from that, love will grow. You are not from another planet, you too can experience the love and connection you need and desire. And if your beloved sourdough bread is unavailable, give a new bread a try; start eating other breads, cultivating new interests, contacts, and connections in life. When you do this, you create new pathways for love to flow into and out of your heart. Instead of being a bottomless pit that sits in the shadows of your own pain and despair waiting to *hopefully* be filled up again by your kids, begin to value the friends, family, neighbors, workmates, and even the acquaintances you already have in your life, and then, reach out and touch the lives of strangers and make new friends and connections. Acknowledge them all; reach out to them; get to know them; cherish them and nurture your relationship with them, and in return, they will cherish and nurture their relationship with you. In that instant—BOOM!—another pathway is born in your heart.

Warning: if you've been surviving on a strict diet of sourdough bread alone, it may be a challenge to adjust to an expanded diet full of newness and variety. For me, although I knew my husband loved me, it was my children's love alone that could make or break me emotionally. Here I had a wonderful man and magnificent friends in my life, but, they were not sourdough bread; they were more like crackers, and in spite of their best efforts, they could not fill me up, that is, until I recognized what I was doing and began the hard work of changing my mental/emotional/social diet, along with the long-standing emotional blueprint which dictated my life and relationships to that point. It is no joke that you must finally learn to love and honor yourself first. If you have low self esteem, taking on the hard work of breaking old, defeating patterns and replacing them with new/healthy ones will indeed be a big challenge, but then, what else do you have to do but feel sorry for yourself and suffer? Why not invest your time and energy in expanding the pathways of your heart and enriching your life? I dare you to grow. C'mon, let's give it a try. Begin to recognize and appreciate your many assets, your inner and outer beauty. Make a list of all the challenges you've taken on and accomplished in life. Remember all those random acts of love and kindness throughout your life. Select happy, empowering memories and immerse yourself in them. Begin to love and care for yourself as you would another, as you would your own child.

Begin to love and parent yourself. Become the parent *(to yourself)* that you always wanted and deserved as a child. Begin to love yourself unconditionally. Take an inventory of who you hang out with and whether they make you feel enriched or enslaved, enlightened or enraged; whether they help you to grow and move in a positive direction in life or whether they hold you back and wallow in pettiness and pain with you. If your current peer group falls into the latter category, release those people from your immediate circle of friends, and if they're too toxic, release them from your life entirely. Choose to surround yourself with people that are balanced and positive, and who want to grow and contribute in life.

Note: You can release people from your life in a loving, non-judgmental way; it is possible, and you need not feel guilty or ashamed for moving past toxic relationships that do not serve a higher purpose in your life or theirs.

Exercise your way to a higher sense of self and self esteem

I strongly encourage you to begin an exercise program of some sort. Start small, with baby steps. I don't care how out of shape, lazy or overweight you are, you can do it! Exercise not only strengthens your body, it also enlivens your self esteem. And as an extra added bonus, it also releases endorphins, a powerful and entirely free source of joy and well being that will aid you tremendously as you journey on your path of self-discovery and personal healing and growth.

I remember the first time I tried to run. I didn't make it to the end of the block. The muscles in my legs burned and I could not breathe. It felt as if my lungs had collapsed as I strained to catch my breath. Dizzy, I stood stooped over on the side walk panting in defeat. Then and there, I gave up and never tried to run again. Instead of challenging myself, I became a couch potato and was rather adept at it, if I do say so myself. Then, as age fifty approached, I took an honest look at myself emotionally and physically and was not happy with what I had become. I was completely emotionally dependent upon my children for my sense of worth and happiness, and they knew it. I was personally unfulfilled and unexpressed as the unique individual Spirit had created and intended me to be. I had no hobbies or interests outside being a super-pleaser/server/fixer/rescuer to my adult children. Food and cable television were my best friends and constant companions. It had happened! I had become a black hole, a bottomless pit that never felt full. It was then and there that I made a decision, a mandate that would change my life. I decided to be rigorously honest with myself and undertook a spiritual/physical fast and cleanse. Although I did nourish myself with fresh vegetable and fruit juices and supplemented my juice-diet with vitamins and minerals, I did not eat solid food of any kind. I read, prayed, and meditated twice a day and with that, created an opening for insights and transformation of my life. I allowed spirit and my own sense of physical well-being to dictate the length of my fast which ended up lasting an incredible fifty days. I lost 36 pounds, but more important than that, I gained powerful insights and had grown exponentially both personally and spiritually. During that process, I had found my bliss, my own source, my soul.

With my newfound sense of self and enlivened spirit, I became determined to give that *running thing* another shot. My initial goal was to run one block, the distance I had miserably failed at two years earlier and I did that. Then it was one-tenth of a mile, then two-tenths and so on. I was elated when I ran a quarter mile for the very first time. I then took up cycling. I remember calling my husband bursting with happiness and pride the first time I rode my bike a whooping seven miles. I was on a roll! Eventually I ran a half mile, then a mile. Running three miles without stopping was a huge milestone for me. Then it happened—five miles! What an incredible feeling of accomplishment. It had been two months since I started running and I was in heaven. I never, not in a million years, dreamt that I'd run five miles. I was on top of the world and felt great about myself in virtually every way. Where before, I hated running, now I found that for me, it had become a moving meditation, a time to pray, meditate, and express my deep appreciation for all the things I was blessed with in my life. I will always remember a rainy fall evening when I ran ten miles for the very first time in my life; that remains one of my happiest, most fulfilling memories. I was at the zenith of personal connection with myself, both in body, mind, and spirit. I had become my own person with my very own identity and the experience was wonderful.

While expanding on my running career, I was also cycling and getting better at that too. With all the strides I had made, I was feeling like a new woman. I had an identity, I had my own source of personal pride, validation and worth that could not be taken away from me and it felt good. Where before, I had been a self-appointed emotional slave, couch potato, and television addict, as my fiftieth birthday approached, I was living a healthy and vibrant life. I was on such a high that I decided that for my fiftieth birthday, I would participate in a triathlon. I trained to swim a quarter of a mile in open water, cycle 12 miles and then run a 5k—all on the same day-in succession! Although it wasn't an Ironman, it was the equivalent of one for me. It was also a far-cry from the woman who had no personal interests or hobbies and couldn't run a short block. When it came time to participate in the triathlon, I was scared to death. I also had no delusions of grandeur; I simply wanted to complete the challenge that lay before me and cross the finish line upright, and finish I did.

I would go on to participate in more triathlons. I also created a *Life Celebration List* (what others might call a 'Bucket List) that included learning to surf in Hawaii, cycling a hundred miles, running 18 miles, cliff jumping, paddle boarding, and swimming two and a-half miles (the official ironman swimming distance). All these adventures and athletic accomplishments were once inconceivable to me and now are just part of *who I am*. I share this story not to impress you but rather to inspire you to take up an interest, a challenge that gets you out of the house and gets your body moving. A healthy emotional and physical diet and exercise are critical to mental and physical health, as well as being a powerful building block to a healthy self-esteem and life-enriching self confidence.

> **Important Note:** *I do not advocate or advise fasting either for weight loss or for any other purpose. If you are interested in the subject of juice fasting, I strongly advise you to educate yourself and consult a physician before undertaking such an endeavor.*

Volunteer

It is so true, that you don't realize how fortunate you are until you see the suffering of others firsthand. If you're lonely and want to create the love and connection you crave, one way to do it is to reach out to others in need. There is no shortage of places to look. There are Veteran's organizations and charities, hospice, children's hospitals, the humane society and other animal sanctuary groups, environmental groups, emergency hotlines, and women's support groups. You can become a mentor or foster parent to a child or take-in or foster an animal in need.

The rewards of being a pet parent

There is one immediate answer to loneliness. If you don't have one, consider getting a pet. The sense of love and connection you get from sharing your life with a dog or a cat is nothing short of amazing. To expound upon the sentiments expressed by one of our parents in chapter three, pets, dogs in particular, are incredibly loyal and forgiving companions who don't talk back or holler at you. They will never lie to you or manipulate you. They never ask for money or the car keys. They don't require medical insurance and you don't have to buy them a car, send them to college, or pay for their wedding. They are always delighted to see you, even when you walk outside to get the mail and come right back. Best of all, all they want from you, is the same thing they're eager to give you, pure, unadulterated love.

The Bottom line

It's a law of the universe that you must *give* the love you crave in your life. Don't wait for it to come to you or magically appear in your life. Go get some of it for yourself. Create it. Seize the day! Grab it with both arms and squeeze tightly. And as you begin to grow and experience new pathways and avenues of love in your heart and life, should you experience moments of regret that you are not presently experiencing and enjoying the love of your child in your life (the love and connection you once defined as your sole means of sustenance) remember that you don't need, want, and should never rely on only one source of nourishment and love in your life in order to be alive and thrive. Reaffirm your love and desire for a healthy connection with your adult child. Pray for them and for healing. Send them your love and if the situation requires it, release them to your higher power during this time of separation. Release all your old beliefs and ways of being and begin to allow the many other manifestations and avenues of love available to you to make their way into your life and heart. And know that these new pathways and experiences are not meant to replace that special love and life force which is your connection to your child, but merely to complete you as a human and spiritual being and fill that void you have created in your heart and life. In the end, growing and expanding, and allowing more pathways for love and new and interesting life experience will ultimately make for a better, more balanced, rewarding, respectful, and reciprocal relationship with your adult child one day. You will be a whole and fulfilled person and parent, and there's nothing more attractive and appealing than being in the company of a strong, self referring, balanced and happy person.

Seeking Spiritual Balance and connection with your higher self

In addition to reconnecting with the emotionally healthy people already in your life, creating new loving connections, getting off your butt and going outside and moving your body, and finding a way to *give back*, it's also important that you reconnect with *Source*— your higher power. I have no intention of being preachy, nor do I claim to have the market cornered on spiritual truth; I only know what it is for me. Hopefully you have a sense of certainty relative to what it is for you too. The bible says *"Seek and ye shall find."* Seek out and develop your own spiritual foundation and faith, then rely upon it. This is so important. I believe it is our ultimate reason for being here and having the experiences we do in this life because *amazing grace* is exactly what God/Source/the Universe provides for you when you rest all your burdens *(those heavy stones)* on your higher power and trust that they're safe at that altar. In this case, if it's your child's behavior or lack of a relationship with them that is causing you pain, regret, or worry, lovingly place them in that higher place and give them over to the care of the creator/universe. Once you are able to do that, you are then given the growth experience of learning to trust that all things will work together for everyone's *ultimate* good, not necessarily their *immediate* good or *'good'* as you or I might perceive or define it, but as *spirit* defines it. That's what *faith* is all about.

Loving unconditionally but sometimes from a distance

Whether you've made the painful but necessary decision to call a time-out or your child has taken their love away, you must stay lovingly strong, maintain your healthy boundaries, and if necessary, continue to love your adult child from a distance.

Be clear—I am not advocating abandoning one's children, nor am I saying that you shouldn't make peace or extend an olive branch. My guess is, you're an expert at forgiving and extending the olive branch, and perhaps it's even been accepted (for awhile) until the next storm arises. What I am referring to are *abusive relationships;* relationships where there has been such an unhealthy power shift, where you are left groveling for any crumbs that may fall from the table; a place where you settle for neglect or make verbal abuse okay. That is absolutely *not* acceptable. That kind of disrespect only breeds more disrespect, contempt, and abuse and usually requires a catalyst for change.

If you're in the middle of such a storm, I encourage you to set reasonable boundaries, communicate them lovingly but adamantly, and then love and respect yourself enough to diligently maintain them because not only are they your self-respect barometers, they are the bridges across which, healthy love will one day return. Let your child know that healthy love and respect that is genuine and mutual is always available to them but that abusive behavior will not be tolerated. If that results in love being taken away, maintain whatever healthy/essential boundaries you've established until mutual love and respect is agreed upon and shared. Key for you is to stop focusing only on your pain. *Focus* is a very obedient beast and is always at *your* command. Wherever your focus and attention go, your thoughts and energy are not far behind. That is why it's imperative that you *not* wallow in loneliness and self pity, rather, expand and grow, create new pathways of love and connection in your life; go out and enjoy new experiences, establish new and challenging life goals. Volunteer, make healthy connections, and finally, entrust your child to your higher power and pray for them.

> *God grant me the serenity to accept the things I cannot change*
> *The courage to change the things I can*
> *And the wisdom to know the difference*

Getting the support you need

Getting the support you need via friends, life coaches, counselors, books, CDs, & seminars is an important ingredient in your new life path. Begin now to create a support system, a network of friends and people with whom you can share special days and events, and lean on when you're feeling weak and vulnerable. Believe it or not, this period of your life can be very healing and rewarding. It can be a time when you grow the most and reconnect with the healthy self-worth and self-esteem you were originally born with and deserve. Start by taking an inventory of the friends and family already in your life, and if you've been sacrificing them on the altar of your own pain, then speak to them, share, and if necessary apologize and make a commitment to create a new and healthy relationship with them. If your marriage has suffered or taken a back seat, it's time to reinvest in it and in your partner. Volunteer or join a church or community group; give back! Someone once wisely said, in order to have friends, one must *be friendly*. After all, remember:

We are the only species on earth that possesses the ability to create love & connection where once there was none, simply because we desire to

Begin today to

- ❖ Concentrate your thoughts and energies in positive, healing directions
- ❖ Change your routine
- ❖ Make new choices
- ❖ Set new goals—set any new goal, even a little one
- ❖ Learn something new about yourself
- ❖ Discover new interests
- ❖ Dare to be adventurous. Do something you've always wanted to do but were too shy, too conservative, too afraid or embarrassed to do
- ❖ If you're selfless and frugal, buy something you've always wanted but didn't want to spend the money on. Spurge! You deserve it.
- ❖ Call or write to someone you haven't spoken to in years
- ❖ Turn the television off and the stereo on
- ❖ Dance
- ❖ Sing
- ❖ Read, learn, grow and expand
- ❖ Get your tush off the couch!
- ❖ Exercise (even if that means walking to the end of the block)
- ❖ Join a club or support group
- ❖ Volunteer. Go visit the frightened, lonely animals at your local animal shelter
- ❖ Grab some magazines and take them (and yourself) to visit elderly folks living facilities, hospices, and retirement homes; they're lonelier than you are and will appreciate your visit.
- ❖ Give back.
- ❖ Get into therapy *(if that's where you're led)*
- ❖ Join a healthy church/spiritual center—develop and nurture your spiritual life
- ❖ Fall in love with *you*
- ❖ Seek wisdom and growth in your life

❖ Pray for your child and send out love daily
❖ Lovingly maintain healthy boundaries in your life
❖ Always remember—you're not alone.

Keep the faith!

CHAPTER 21

A Word for Husbands & Partners

You men are goal/action-oriented, problem solving beings. You want to fix what's broken and move on. Likewise, *if it isn't broken—don't mess with it* is also a tenet of manhood. I'd hazard a bet that the last thing you want to do is become immersed in layers and layers of family drama; and you certainly don't want to talk about it, read about it, or dwell upon it every waking moment—right? Good, glad we agree. And just so you know, I'll bear that in mind and keep this chapter short and to the point.

Men in general are great at *letting things go,* whereas most women, especially mothers, are all about probing and analyzing their *"feelings"* and not just *their* feelings, oh no, they're worried and concerned about your feelings, the children's feelings, *her* extended family's feelings, *your* extended family's feelings, her friends feelings, her friend's-friend's feelings, the neighbor's feelings, and to your utter amazement, the dog's feelings too. Hell, you've actually watched in astonishment as she worried and speculated over the behavior of complete strangers before. Am I right? Guys, newsflash, it's an engineering glitch. In other words, it's just the way we're built and there's not a whole hell of a lot you can do about it. But that's not entirely bad news. Knowledge and insight equal power; that means it's *good* that you're taking a moment to learn a little bit about your wife and partner, and how she's hardwired. Think of a mother as a shark. If she stops, she dies. I can tell you firsthand, as mothers, we are constantly in motion, mentally, emotionally and/or physically, and usually we're engaged in all three arenas at once when it comes to our family and our concern for their well being. We are constantly planning for, or doing all we can for our children and/or grandchildren. Even when it doesn't look like we are in motion because we appear still, we are thinking, planning, contemplating, calculating, anticipating, worrying, or praying. Another thing, and you probably already know this—*Women Never Forget*. And I mean NEVER! Men forget things all the time, and usually before they're supposed to (at least according to us women). The good news is, you can blame this deficiency on hardwiring and brain chemistry; like women, it's just the way *you're* hardwired.

Research has revealed that women are the thinker, worrier, feeler, talker of our species and that they use both sides of the brain at the same time, almost all the time. That means that for women, everything is not just a cognitive function, it's an emotional affair as well. Men do not function that way. Men are left-brain dominate when it comes to communication; that means they're more objective, rational and less emotionally involved with or attached to the material they are sending out or receiving. For women, just about everything they encounter holds the potential of being a highly charged emotional experience. In short, we experience and process life quite differently. Of course there are men who are in touch with their right brain/feminine side (they are the men who will voluntarily read the entire book without being begged, threatened or cajoled).

Humor aside, what's important to remember is that women are strikingly different than men. We don't process things the way you do. We feel and experience things quite differently. We worry, fret and hover. We make mountains out of a mole hills. We feel and need to talk about everything and never forget anything. On the bright side, those same traits are what make us awesome wives, mothers, and caregivers. They are also part of the reason you fell in love with your lady in the first place. Because we think and feel things so thoroughly and deeply, we naturally take on everyone else's needs and problems and become heroically committed to them. We then focus on, worry about, and sometimes obsess about other people's feelings, intentions, actions, needs, and desires. What destroys us at times is also what makes us so amazing; it's that same doggedness that drives your wife to make sure you see the doctor, take your medication, eat properly, give up smoking or an array of other things she feels it's her duty to oversee, worry about, and accomplish for you and her family. It's also why we were designated to be the gender to take on pregnancy and birth, and the primary responsibility of parenting *(protecting and nurturing)* but I suspect you already knew that.

You know all too well that the woman you love went through nine months of discomfort and pregnancy. You know this not only because there is a child that is direct evidence of the event but also because she's shown you the stretch marks! She's talked about the morning sickness; and Lord knows everyone has heard about her labor and birthing experience. She complains about her womanliness being destroyed or at least deflated, and again, you know this because she's shown you the scars, usually in tears. Or, if she's too embarrassed, ashamed, or afraid of your rejection, she's gone out of her way to camouflage her flaws, or hide the scars of motherhood from you. Whether she hides or reveals them, you know that for life, this incredible woman carries with her constant reminders of her commitment to another human being's life. That living monument is composed of the physical scars of motherhood she bears, and they must be honored. By the way, although the scars may have disfigured a once pristine young body and wounded her female self-esteem, she wouldn't trade them for anything in the world, not if it meant never holding her baby in her arms. Children too, need to know this about the wonderful, courageous woman who is their mother.

From the point of conception to the moment when the last bird flies the nest, good mothers give their all, and when the hands-on primary job is done, they often feel abandoned, empty, and depressed because their children do not need them as they once did. In worst case scenarios, certain family dynamics can result in an abusive or neglectful environment for mom. When such unfortunate and painful events unfold, know that it is a life altering, emotionally devastating ordeal for your wife. For you, it may be *just a phase* the kids are going through or you may be able to just scoff it off and say *"the hell with em"* when your teen or adult children is not behaving in a respectful manner, but for your wife/their mother (that woman with the monumental scars of motherhood) it can be an emotionally debilitating crisis. It is also the time when the woman you know has taken care of everyone else and has put everyone else's needs before her own, is now in dire need of some hands-on, heart-felt, love and attention, and you are just the one to give it to her.

You two may have let the kids run the show, or maybe you just sat back and watched the disaster unfold. Whatever the case, it's likely that you two haven't made your coupleship and cultivating a life together your number one priority. That is part of the reason she's so lost right now. You two are supposed to be each other's best friend and anchors in the storm, each other's island of love and sanity, but if that hasn't been your history, then she will be tossed and turned emotionally as she navigates this storm alone and tries to get her bearings. If your wife is in the midst of such a storm, that usually means that the kids were her anchor for years and now that line has been cut and she's adrift in an emotional torrent and desperately needs your help to weather the storm and make it to a safe harbor.

Man Hint: your love and support is the safe harbor and shelter she needs.

Oh, and by the way, as if all that wasn't enough . . .

God or Mother Nature must have one hellevah sense of humor and incredibly dry wit because periods, pregnancy, childbirth, child-rearing, and survival of the tween and then teen years apparently were not enough for your wife to brave and survive. Nope, mother nature thought it'd make things much more interesting for women *(and you too)* if during this incredibly stressful and turbulent time in life, your wife also experienced a little personal hell called *peri-menopause*, followed by the real deal, full-blown heat-flashin', mood swingin', sexually deficient, irritable-as-hell *menopause*. I think they call it **'men-o-pause'** because it gives full-grown men reason to pause and wonder *'what the hell is going on?''Where did the woman*

I love disappear to?' and *'Who is this sweaty, sexless, shrew who keeps messin' with the thermostat every night?'*

Gentlemen and partners, menopause is not a fun-fest for you, we know this, but what *you* must accept and brand into your mind is the reality that it no *walk in the park* for your wife either, in fact, it can be an agonizing nightmare that robs her of her sense of well-being, femininity, sleep, emotional balance and joy. It is an uninvited, unwelcome \$#%★ load of physical and emotional stress that, although separate from, most definitely aggravates and exacerbates the stress she is already experiencing as a result of dealing with ill-behaved or neglectful adult children while simultaneously trying to find her place in the world.

For your wife, this time of life can constitute a triple threat. So please, try to remember that along with family stress and drama, mid-life changes, and the physical scars and infirmities she may carry on the outside, many mothers also have inside wounds and scars too; places where they hurt deeply. Places where they feel misunderstood or under-appreciated either by you, by the kids, or both. Those wounds arise when a good (and perhaps needy) mother makes it her life's purpose to love, please, serve, fix, and rescue her teen or adult children constantly and unconditionally. When mothers decide to do that, they potentially set themselves up for a tremendous amount of pain in the long run. Many times, when that happens, it also means that you've taken a back seat to the kids for years too. Maybe you're okay with that, or maybe you put the kids first too/maybe not, I don't know. But one thing is for sure, as the kids get older, it is important that *you two* take back the keys to your life, get your butts back in the front seat where they belong, and start driving in the *same* direction—together!

So what's a Good Husband to do?—Here's a 'Honey Do' list

✓ Just listen. That's a wonderful gift you can give for free and requires. no action. Your wife doesn't expect you to solve everything for her; she just needs you to listen to her, and when you do . . .

✓ Be supportive and show that you genuinely care for her *(even if it's not like you to do so)*.

✓ Encourage her.

✓ Touch her tenderly and thoughtfully, and for more than 30 seconds.

✓ Hold her, and not just when you want sex or have bad news to share.

✓ Acknowledge her wonderful traits and values, and sincerely compliment her on them.

✓ Thank her for being a mother and for being your wife.

✓ Together set healthy boundaries and goals relative to your relationship, parenthood, acquaintances & friendships, etc.

✓ Make your relationship priority one. *And if she needs or wants you to—*

✓ Accompany her to counseling. If she asks, say *"yes"* Remember the stretch marks and scars! If she deems counseling as necessary for her stability and emotional growth, your sacrifice in this department will be small compared to the sacrifices she's made for you and the kids, and if you doubt it, ask her to show you her scars again.

✓ Love each other unconditionally.

✓ Set a date night, and keep it

✓ Send your sweetheart a card or flowers, just because . . .

✓ Ask her to marry you all over again, and do it.

✓ Be more intimate; make it a priority, and if necessary, calendar it

✓ Learn new things about each other, as well as your separate and shared interests.

✓ Do something different than what you're both accustomed to; create new adventures and memories together.

✓ Be her Rock! Don't let her sit and stew. Break up her pattern and habit of victimhood.

✓ Get out of the house and get moving.

✓ Lay a blanket on the beach or in the woods, put on a romantic CD, open a bottle of wine and experience a sunset together.

✓ Share a secret no one else knows about you.

✓ Remind her that tremendous growth and great good can come from this, but only if you are willing to create an opening for it to happen.

That's it. Congratulations! You made it through these few pages written especially for husbands and partners. Thank you for letting me share with you what most women and especially mothers want, need, and deserve from their partners. I encourage you take on the challenge of embodying the love, strength, and support your wife, friend, and partner needs, both now and into the future. I also hope you will read the entire book, not only will it impress the hell out of your lady and make her feel special and important, it will give you additional insights into what makes her tick and why she's trapped in the hell she is. By the way, the book is also a map that will show you where she's been, how she got there, and most importantly—the road out. And whatever you do, don't forget your *honey-do list*. You can start off by closing this book and thanking your wife for being open and vulnerable enough to share with you; then hold her and ask her what she needs from you right now.

—The Beginning—

About the Author

Kay Taylor is in a unique position to understand human behavior and the inner-personal struggles and relationship dynamics and challenges that modern life and parenthood presents. Having lived with over a hundred foster children during her formative and teen years, and being married off at the age of sixteen and then raising two children alone while working two jobs and attending college, Ms. Taylor offers a unique and insightful view of what it's like to be mother, working single parent, and stepmother to what she refers to as E-generation children (children who compete with their parents for power and control). Professionally, Ms. Taylor worked as a staff writer for a national magazine and later as a freelance writer for several newspapers, television, and commercial print media. After a successful career in corporate America later in her life, Ms. Taylor retired to Florida where she and her husband Neil enjoy boating, cycling, and time spent with family, friends, and their beloved dogs and parrot Kahlua, who Kay and Neil jokingly refer to as the only children they've had together. In Free Mother to Good Home, Kay Taylor speaks to new millennia challenges from a parent's perspective, as well as from the place from which all human needs arise—the heart. And from that sacred place, she addresses the human need and desire to experience self awareness, self respect, and authentic love and connection.

CPSIA information can be obtained at www.ICGtesting.com
Printed in the USA
BVOW08s1745060316

439284BV00001B/48/P